THE PANDEMIC CHRONICLES

Volume I

First Printing, 2022

ISBN: 979-8-218-05225-6

King James Version Scripture quotations marked "KJV" are taken from the Holy Bible, King James Version (Public Domain).

Message Bible Version Scripture quotations marked "MSG" are taken from the Holy Bible, Message Bible (Public Domain).

New International Version Scripture quotations markets "NIV" are taken from the Holy Bible, New International Bible (Public Domain).

Publisher:
Autore
Wilmington, DE
www.mioautore.com

DEDICATION

I want to dedicate this book to my husband Frank, our children, my community of mentees/spiritual children, the body of Christ at large, readers, prophetic company's, families, businesses, and to all the families who lost loved ones during the trying times of the Pandemic. My heart goes out to you.

TABLE OF CONTENTS

FOREWORD

BY DR. NAIM COLLINS

Dr. Felicia Brown, in her phenomenal book *The Pandemic Chronicles,* has interwoven the prophetic penmanship and authorship of those who share with us how they overcame every challenge, obstacle, and struggle during the most unforeseen global pandemic in the modern era. This book is not your ordinary book, but rather a chronicle of the testimonies and the power of God manifested in those who survived during the darkest hour.

The power of God revealed with each authors' impactful story confirms the very words in Revelation 12:11:

> *"And they overcame him because of the blood of the Lamb, and because of the word of their testimony;"*

Each story was specially written with you and me in mind. It is a compilation and memoir penned by some extraordinary women. As I read through each chapter, I was literally moved to tears hearing the different personal testimonies of physical and health issues, managing all kinds of addiction, depression, financial struggles, social and family isolation, fear, anxiety, and stress that were all triggered by the

COVID-19 pandemic. With all that has happened over the past two years you will, to some degree or another, be able to relate to one or all the stories.

Dr. Felicia has coordinated a body of work in this literary masterpiece to track and capture the vulnerabilities, traumas, and life-altering experiences of these women in similar fashion to how Moses the prophet was tasked to write and chronicle a memorial and commemoration for the children of Israel and successive generations, the various events, works and testimonies of God, bringing them out of Egypt (Exodus 13:3). This book: *The Pandemic Chronicle* is a MUST read for anyone who has been impacted spiritually, personally, financially, emotionally, professionally, or economically by the series of events presented by this deadly virus that has literally changed our way of life and its quality.

What you hold in your hands is the true stories of anointed writers who, through the power of love and transparency, invite us into their lives. It will consequently inspire, encourage, empower, and provoke you to trust the God of the impossible to bring you through the insurmountable. The very titles of each chapter in volume one of this book will become a lifeline and umbilical cord to revive you and birth to push you through your struggles. I believe these are God inspired: *The Pursuit of God; The Beginning, The Power of a Word; Developing in the Dark; In Pursuit to Push; The Pandemic Taught Me to Trust Again; I Weather the Storm; Miracles in Perseverance; Trust the Plan; The Divine Start; Birthing Pains in Time and Space; and 14-Days Living with Covid-19.*

God has given Dr. Felicia Brown the vision in this power-packed book to speak to all of us who have lost a loved one or who are presently dealing with the aftermath and residual effects of this pandemic. A pandemic that was demonically sent to disrupt and distract us from the plans of God. Most inspiring were he words that jumped off the pages to speak life in the midst of death, healing in the middle of calamity, peace in the eye of the storm, and hope in the center of hopelessness. These twelve heroes have released a diversity of an anointing in this book that will give you the formidable grace and power to SURVIVE (Zephaniah 3:17)!

Dr. Naim Collins
President of League of the Prophets
Author of *Realms of the Prophetic and Power Prophecy*
Wilmington, Delaware USA

INTRODUCTION

To say the coronavirus (COVID-19) pandemic changed our way of life would be an understatement. Less than a year after the virus emerged — and just over 6 months after tracking began in the United States — it upended day-to-day lives across the world. The pandemic has changed how we work, learn, and interact. Social distancing guidelines have led to an increasing virtual existence personally, professionally, and spiritually.

Surveys have revealed that as a result of the pandemic, Americans have changed how they approach their overall health and health care in both positive and negative ways. Unsurprisingly, the pandemic has triggered a wave of mental health issues… managing addiction, depression, social isolation, fear, and stress. When public health mandates limited in-person gatherings beginning in March 2020, a significant change and consequent challenge for many churches occurred, moving worship services as well as other elements of church life online. Church fellowship is a staple, and a lifeline, if you will, in the lives of believers, especially during difficult times, thus pandemic restrictions forced churches to adapt to doing ministry work without actually being able to meet in person.

Welcome to a Mentor and Mentees' memoir of our life stories during the pandemic and how we overcame every challenge with God's help in victory through prayer, fasting, the word, and divine instructions. When you read these true-life stories, slow down, listen to the words in your heart as well as your mind. Let them encourage you. Let them revive and refresh you, let them touch you at the point of your need. I have no doubt you will relate to one or all these stories that come straight from our heart to yours. These powerful women pour out their experience during the pandemic and the effect it had on their families, bodies, employment, and mind. Some stories will make you laugh, some will make you cry, some will cause an aha moment, and some may make you dance. There is no right, or wrong reaction, just let it happen.

You are a survivor!

THE BEGINNING

I can remember hearing a report about a virus while listening to the news. It was a brief segment, not much to it. I hadn't really watched or listened much to the news over the previous few years. I would only catch a few minutes on the local news station in my car on the way to work in the morning. I would read some social media posts or email notifications. I don't know at what point I started to pay attention to what was being said, but I do know I started feeling like I needed to do certain things. I started to modify the way I shopped for groceries and the way I purchased food.

Although, I changed my diet several years ago because of food challenges, I knew that I still needed to make more changes. This is still an ongoing process for me even now. I was eating more fresh vegetables and less processed foods. I tried to get creative by replacing ingredients and making substitutes for things that I could no longer eat. It was always an adventure to make something that I liked and that tasted good. I found myself having to go to the grocery store every other day to pick up something for dinner.

I also found myself not going out to eat as much or attend functions that involved me having to eat something from a potluck that someone else cooked. It is cumbersome and gets old trying to explain to people what you can eat and what you can't. I'd rather not go, or just not participate. Sometimes, it gets embarrassing, trying to politely decline. Most people mean well, but they just don't understand. People can get offended or think you're bogus when you are just trying to protect yourself and stay well.

Anyway, with the changes that I was making I needed to find other places to shop. I renewed my big box club membership that had expired two years prior. As I became familiar with the store again, things started to change in the news about what was happening in Europe concerning COVID-19. In the three years leading up to the pandemic, I had had enough of church as usual. I had had enough of going to church and not seeing any progress in my personal and spiritual life. I was recovering from a failed marriage for way too long, and I was broken. I had lost my way.

I was looking for purpose and destiny in my life. I was searching for answers and was not getting them at church, no offense to the ministry, but I needed a change. The change that I needed had to start with me… on the inside of me. I began to cry out to God. As much as I could, I avoided everything that required my attention. I decided not to take on any new projects or ministry. I think that lasted about one year or so. Then, a dear friend of mine asked me to help "work the altar" in her annual ministry conference. I reluctantly agreed. I thought to myself, I will do my best, but I really hope that I will not have to pray for anyone. Coincidently, and serendipitously, that was where I really needed to be.

God had a surprise waiting for me on that day. That surprise was in the form of a human angel. That angel was, Prophetess Felicia A. Brown. She was the keynote speaker. I don't remember her message or her topic, I just remember what happened to me after she prayed for me. At the end of her sermon, she made an altar call. She prayed for all the workers. I was standing up front with everyone at the altar. There was a young man assisting her, he prayed for me first. He laid hands on me and began to minister to me. Looking back, I felt like he was the anesthesiologist that was preparing me for the operation that was about to happen. As he prayed for me, I fell to the floor in worship because my heart began to beat again. God had not forgotten about me. Then, like a whirlwind, she approached me. She ministered to me so accurately, it was exactly what I needed at that time in my life.

I felt like I was on the operating table and God had used her as a surgeon to operate on me. He used her to see what was wrong with my heart, what needed to be done to fix it. God used this Woman of God. That day, God let me know He still had a plan for my life. That surprise set me on the right path. My heart started to recover, and my spirit became realigned. It was only after this experience that I was able to move forward with my life. Thank you to two awesome women of God, Dr. Felicia Brown and Prophetess Cathy Emerson. Their obedience to God saved my life back then. I am truly thankful to God!

In the journey moving forward, I sought my heavenly Father. I started to dream again. I started "to see" and hear what God was saying about me and others even though it was a lot to comprehend. With that being said, in the years that followed, I knew I was becoming more like what he actually called me to be. I began to understand more of who and what I am. I am God's Seer. As strange as it may sound, knowing what God was calling me to, I became more fed up with church than ever. Please understand that I am not just speaking of a particular church, but the church at large. I wanted the kingdom of God to come to earth in the body of Christ. I could no longer put up with charades, pomp and circumstance. I couldn't accept what I called "church shenanigans." I was chasing after God.

I wanted to see the promises of God come to pass in my life. I wanted to see people healed, delivered, and set free. I grew weary watching and waiting for God to move. Not only my family, but in the lives of everyone that I encountered. I wanted to see people receive the healing and deliverance that they needed. I wanted the kingdom of God to come to the earth as it was written in the bible. I know that I am not the only one that has had the experience of attending a church service only to return home feeling empty. Honestly, there were times that I felt like I should have just stayed home. Even though I was dissatisfied in that manner, I continued to pray and seek God. I didn't backslide. I fell on my face.

Needless to say, I did not know that this path was leading me. It was preparing to take me straight into the pandemic. It involved me learning all that I could about my gift *to see* and *dream* and endeavor to understand what *the kingdom of God* was really about. For most of my Christian life, this portion of my walk with God was veiled to me and I could not see clearly. It was an area of my spirit that was dormant and untapped. However, God put people in my path to help guide me.

I began to learn a lot about the prophetic because God put me in the company of other prophetic people. This was amazing to me. While I was learning and growing, and before the pandemic was on the international radar, God began to instruct our small group to pray and prepare in ways that we did not fully understand. We were obedient. We had the benefit of having virtual classes a whole year before everyone started realizing they needed ways to gather and have fellowship. We were being prepared for the pandemic through prayer and fasting.

Let me be clear about this, it wasn't until I humbled myself in prayer that God began to illuminate my path forward. I didn't realize that the changes he was making in me would lead me into a prophetic presbytery. In the years that I was trying to get myself together, our church had developed a prophetic institute that was led by no other than Prophetess Felicia Brown. Does this sound like a shameless plug? Good, because it is. If my aforementioned experience had not occurred, I really don't know where my life would be right now. I just know that it would not be good. God has a way of giving us a lifeline through people. He will use others to help get you to where he wants you if you let him. They are our destiny helpers. Is there a destiny helper in your life?

Getting back to my dissatisfaction with the "church," like so many others that I know, I used to wonder why we were not seeing the miraculous healings taking place, why were people being tormented by devils, afflictions and illnesses? Why was I not doing "greater" works? These signs should follow me because I believe, right? What was I doing wrong? What was the church doing wrong?

As I am writing this, I realize that my dissatisfaction with the church was not just "my dissatisfaction." It wasn't just my burden or a feeling of disappointment that I was internalizing. This is what God was feeling himself the whole time for his church. It was God tugging at my heart strings. It was His pain that made me feel sad. I see people in pain that can't help themselves, or someone with an incurable disease. What about the times that someone had a monetary need, or even something that money can't buy, like a broken heart?

These are all God's feelings toward us. He wants us to be whole and healed. He wants us to have his peace in every area of our lives. He wants his kingdom to come on the earth just like it is in heaven. How do we know this? We know this because he was wounded for our transgressions and bruised for our iniquities. (Isaiah 53: 112 MSG) We know this also because he has come to give us an abundant life. (John 10:6-13 MSG)

Jesus preached and taught about the kingdom of God. In his ministry on earth, he healed the sick, he raised the dead, he fed the hungry. He brought the message of the Kingdom to the earth. He taught his disciples to do the same but told them that they would do greater things than what he did himself while he was amongst them. This is what our heavenly Father wants for us today.

When reading the Gospels and taking in what Jesus did during his ministry on the earth, and then comparing those things to how we live and function as believers today, one should be able to see why God is grieved with the "church" of today.

I discovered in my own walk with God that what I want for my life, my family, the church, and the body of Christ is what God wants. His kingdom to come on earth like it is in Heaven. I have most certainly realized that I don't want to waste another day going through pomp and circumstance, church shenanigans and otherwise. I can see why there is a need to reset the church. God was looking for his kingdom in his people, but we were not looking for him. He couldn't find himself in our programs, in our worship, in our offerings, and sadly, not enough in our hearts. Interestingly, just as the world needs to repent, so does the church. Now that the world has had to literally shut down, we should have more time to reflect and repent. Unfortunately, so many people did not have that chance. Before the shutdown took place, I was on a quest to find my purpose and my destiny. It was my desire for His kingdom to come on the earth, and it still is.

I have realized that more people are now searching for their purpose and destiny. Some have repented and turned back to God. Many churches have had to change their format while others have completely folded. In the days to come, we will see the church come to the forefront. We will see the kingdom of God arise on earth. We will see signs, miracles and wonders, as in the bible, even things that we cannot explain, only that God did it. Those of us who have been seeking, searching and waiting will see the manifestation of his glory. We do not have to wait any longer. The time is now.

Although this pandemic has brought out the worst and the best of people, it is still God's will that people repent and turn to him. So many people need to answer the call in their lives. They need to hear the word of the Lord. They need to hear the Good News of the Gospel of Jesus Christ. This pandemic has brought me to the place that I am searching for. That place is a rise of his glory on earth, a manifestation of his power through us, the believers.

Elder Tyeast Amankwah

THE POWER OF
THE SPOKEN WORD

There are times when we struggle with a word that has been spoken over our lives with our circumstances and desires that have not happened yet… in our timing. The process of waiting for the manifestation or breakthrough can be frustrating. God is not slack, late, nor silent concerning his promises. They are in him yes and amen. Sometimes we allow our discernment to be tainted by what our natural eyes see, and minds understand. This focus can rob us of that pure seed planted in our hearts by the spirit. We must trust God with the seeds that he plants in us, his words over us are wrapped in his faithful promises and never-ending love. It will require the softness of our hearts to grow deep roots and break through the ground of Faith so that the seeds will manifest in the earthly realm. We cannot demand how and when God will grow or manifest that seed, or even when it will move from soil to the visible realm. We must allow the roots to go deep so that when trouble comes, or circumstances look contrary to the word, our seed will not be plucked up while still in its tender stages, the beginnings. God might only show you a piece or glimpse of it on purpose, for the word of God says in I Corinthians 13:9. "For we know in part, and we prophesy in part… he may not show the whole picture or your next steps until you walk in obedience and take a step of faith on the word spoken you." Many times, as believers we're told when God tells you to do something, obviously you do it. But sometimes that's easier said than done, and it's complicated because God's voice often sounds like our own good ideas. Sometimes God will tell you to do something that will have you question whether you heard him or not, the thing is, God may have something greater and better down the road for you, he has our best interests at heart, and he might not show you what all those details are until you take step out on faith. Often, he'll hide the details of the next step from us so that we can fully rely on him and not try to mess with (we think improve) his plan. Jeremiah 29:11 says: "For I know the plans I have for you, declares the Lord, plans to prosper you and not to harm you, plans to give you hope and a future." So, allow that seed to be proven it fell on good ground. You ask what good ground is, Prophet? Thanks for asking, in Luke 8:15, the bible talks about the word (seed) falling on good soil, good ground, which refers to someone who hears the word in honesty and good heart (soft heart, surrendered heart) and understands it, this is the one who will produce a crop, yielding a hundred, sixty or thirty times what was sown. I stop to prophesize that as you hear the authentic word of God spoken to you, you will obey the voice of the Lord and Deuteronomy 1:11 will be your reality. May the Lord, the God of your fathers, make you a Thousand times greater in number than you are, and give you, his blessings.

Follow me as I share with you how important it is to hear and obey God. I remember the day so clearly, as if it was yesterday. My husband and I had met someone who shared with us an important piece of information regarding our business, we had no idea we had missed it. With this wisdom and instruction, we had received, we began revisiting, readjusting, resetting, and amending our articles of incorporation and business credentials for larger capacity and expansion. We were so excited how the Lord had begun orchestrating the whole thing. I began fleecing God about strategic ways to help my husband and I find ways to make it easier to get the business part of things done financially. I began pulling out and dusting off my resumes, lol! With the skills, talents, and abilities I had surely, I could go back to work. So, I began searching for nursing jobs preferably private duty, or one-on one assignments in my area. My daughter was working for an agency in Maryland and referred me. I was overjoyed to be hired on the spot based solely on my background in nursing and an outdated license. I took a nursing test and passed with flying colors. I began working with one client, 4 days a week. I really enjoyed what I was doing, being back in the nursing field was my passion. After a few months, I felt like I was missing something, I didn't understand why I was feeling the way I was with the good money I was making, and able to pay for all the business fees, licenses, and startup costs etc. I began to pray about the feelings I was having, and the Lord spoke to my spirit about my search not being over, that this wasn't the job, and that I wouldn't be doing this long, there was another opportunity waiting for me that would give me the experience and tools I would need for our business. My nursing assignment had come to an end sooner than the original time planned. It lasted only 3 months. I kept searching, and out of the blue, one night I was on Facebook, I saw one of our church members post a position opening for an administrator's assistant job, the applicant would be her personal assistant. I asked one of my mentees from my church to put me in contact with her, and she did. I went to church that Sunday and spotted her. Yup, I didn't let up until I talked to her. Smiling, I walked over to her, introduced myself, and told her I was interested and would like to apply for the position. I was confident and bold, "honey," she just stared at me with this blank stare, "what position?" I was like, "what the world? Lol, the one you posted on Facebook about the admin assistant job." She had posted it some months ago and took it down, she didn't even know how I had even seen it. Not only that, one of her family members had responded to the post and wanted the job. I was persistent, like the women in the bible with the unjust judge (laughing). I said, "but did she apply and get the job?" And she said actually "No." Nevertheless, that was my cue to say, "I'll come apply when you need me to, I'm available!" Well, she told me that she was on her way to work right after church and her office wasn't too far from the church. I not only filled out the application, but she also ended up interviewing me on the spot. My God! I could not believe how fast and smooth this was going. I would be working for the state, and it would prove to be greatly beneficial. Because I was still on call for nursing assignments, I called the agency to let them know I would no longer be available to work, which was my two-week notice. Needless to say, I got the job after a second interview. Before I picked my start date, my husband and I prayed over the job and decided that I would follow the plan and assignment God had now given me. I asked the Lord to show me my assignment and to whom I was assigned to and show me that I would be a good fit in this new position. He ended up showing me that I was going to be like a midwife to her, as she was my boss, and also like an armor bearer is to a pastor but in corporate world. My last question was how long I would be there. I wanted to fulfill my purpose, not leaving without everything I needed to learn and not staying longer than I was supposed to. He started revealing things about the office, things that had taken place before I was even there, he revealed things about the grounds our offices were built on. He told me to tell my boss that what she was waiting on for the last twenty years was now over. The wait was over, she was now in transition for promotion, get ready, it was happening in the next thirty days. The Lord gave her a few instructions and she followed them out to the letter.

Everything began to change immediately. Within those thirty days, she was promoted to be the first African American woman to be in such an elevated position in our job. Glory be to God for the things He has done. I was not expecting this, but they asked me to apply and step into her position as she left our park to serve in another as assistant superintendent. I told them that I would pass on the position, I was only there temporarily. Little did we know that this change would affect both of us. Do not let me forget to mention, I took the job at $9.00 dollars an hour (smiling) and I was at peace in the lowest paying job I have ever had.

The nursing agency owner ended up calling me to say they needed me for a new assignment, they knew I would work well for the clients. I told her I had started working full time and couldn't. Well, she offered me $20 dollars more than I was already making. Can you believe that? That would put me over the amount I needed to fulfill the assigned purpose and get the money we needed for our business. I started adding up how long it would take me to get everything done for the business, dancing and praising about how quickly it could happen. Also, I would do ministry like the Lord told us. I shared this with my husband because he is a man of the word and wisdom, my sounding board to keep me grounded. I honestly believe this time he thought I was crazy, but his love covered my multitude of crazy (smiling). We talked it out, and I shared my concern, which was it would be obvious to take the higher road, making good money, but it would wear my body down after a while. The lower road or low paying job would give us the inside experience, skills, knowledge, connections, and benefits of sharpening my administrative skills as well as learning the role of office manager, payroll etc. This state job proved to be more beneficial than nursing. After I turned to the nursing job, I kept wondering in my head, "am I doing the right thing? Is this God or me? Am I making something out of nothing? Is this Memorex or live?"

So, I stayed with the state job. When I got to work, different managers or park supers would ask me about taking the position. I really enjoyed what I was doing, and the training was great, that's all I wanted to do. I enjoyed picking the brain of many workers about this whole Parks and Recreation industry. I was really intrigued by it and how they ran things. I had only been there two months when they convinced me to apply for the position. I didn't think I knew enough and hadn't finished all my training. So, I began studying up on everything I needed to know about the office and started looking for ways I could add solutions. Being proactive and innovative in my skills I used for my business and church right there in the office turned out to be a plus. I kept asking myself, "if this is temporary, why am I going along with all this?" After talking with my husband again, then my old boss, I felt a peace about it. I went from $9.00 an hour to a $30,000 raise in two months. As soon as I switched over, there ended up being another $1000 raise that hit our accounts. The Lord is good and faithful!

Let me go back to when I prayed about how long I would be working for this organization. He gave me until July 2020. I was now the new Administrative Specialist II manager of two offices and had two admin assistants under me in two separate offices. This brought out so much creativity and managing skills, along with the knowledge of how to keep office employees on the same page with differences and challenges. Wow! This was going so well that after time went on, I forgot about what the Lord had said to me. I was putting in the work, getting my extra educational credits, and compiled a large folder of all my certificates of training. I was in it to win it! I can see how I was strategically in a place to change and charge the atmosphere. I began cooking for our holiday parties I put together, and boy oh boy, I became caterer to other office employees' events. I was known for my fried chicken, mac & cheese, corn bread, and my banana/strawberry pudding. As you can see, this was the ordained place for me.

Another raise ended coming at the beginning of 2020. I had already changed my mind, saying I am just going finish out 2021 then stop as the Lord leads. Hello! As the Lord leads, seriously? He had already spoken told me what to do. I put myself right in the way, that's how we do things. We forget what he said when things are going really well, we get accustomed to a status quo and start depending on self. Well, the Lord had spoken to me July 2020. I tried to do my own revision of the plans.

It wasn't until right before COVID-19 hit that things started happening in the office, there was a shift of small fires, sabotages and side conversations, things being said, of what I did and what I didn't do. I confronted the issues and exposed the lies. That still didn't change it. My office became a place of tension and strife. The fires I put out before with ease were no longer as easily extinguishable. "What have I done God? What is happening? I am doing what you sent me to do, that devil is trying to mess with my money, he is a liar! Oh yes, he is!" (Lol), was my rant loud and wrong? That was when I went back to really praying again, telling God about the unfairness, lies, knit picking and sabotage, and I had the nerve to ask him to deal with those devils coming, against his child, me, a king's kid, a prophet of the most high God, and I got nothing back not a word. It's like the father was probably saying:" Is she serious right now or nah?" For a minute, it came to my mind, "oh man! Come on God! Did you really say this or was that me trying to make excuses not to leave?"

While we were out of the offices for Covid, a lateral position came into play that would put me 5 minutes from my house... I put in for that lateral and asked myself, "is this what the Lord was talking about?" I wasn't going to be in Wilmington anymore, but I could still work with the state. Hallelujah! Thank you, Lord, for revealing your word was my new rant now still trying to make it work to stay.

Covid-19 was running through the nation, and he reminded me my time was still up, no matter which office I went to, it was not going to work. He reminded me of timing he used a Prophet all the way from Tallahassee, Florida remind me of his word. She was supposed to be setting up an appointment that ran into an issue and that call turned into a God appointment just for me. I was now willing to submit to his will and do what he created me to do on earth with tears in my eyes, I gave God my yes. The lateral went through and as soon as I got to that office, I began getting sick, back-to-back with upper respiratory infections that had never happened before. Then it led to vertigo (who tigo? Lol). Yes, it was so bad that I would go into work and had to immediately leave to go home. You would not believe what month this all started happening. It was July 2020. I was now accused of having covid-19 and people were afraid to be around me in the office so, they made me go for testing, and the result eventually came back negative. I was still out. When I returned, the same thing started again. Needless to say, I clearly remember what the Lord said. It was July 28th, 2020, and I still haven't been back to work. Covid-19 pushed me right out of my comfort zone. What happens NOW....

Dr. Felicia A. Brown

THE DIVINE START

In the summer of 2019, the *divine ball* started to roll! I could sense that some magnificent things were about to happen, and they did! What should have taken years, literally took weeks and months. In July, a Catholic organization paid for my New Jersey substitute certification, something I had wanted for a long time. To me, the certification, was a *ram in the bush* for the start of many things to come. With the cert, I gained part-time employment in public schools, teaching grades K to twelve.

At the end of August, my friend Carol asked if I wanted to go to the shore to allow her daughter to breathe in the ocean air to clear up some bronchitis. I said, "sure." It was then that I realized I had not gone to the shore in almost three years. First, we went to Asbury Park Beach in Monmouth County, NJ. It had a boardwalk and amusement rides and games. While there, we enjoyed the sun and some pizza. As we were leaving, she asked, "do you want to go again tomorrow?" I said, "sure!" Well, to my surprise, we went to a different beach, called Belmar, a 1.3-mile beach featuring a long boardwalk and surfing. It was a chic residential community where the setting looked like something out of a movie. I had seen some beautiful shore-front homes before, but this place, by comparison, was better than them all. The homes had different architectural designs, and each had pristine landscaping. Mind you, I've lived in New Jersey for over forty years, and although I had heard of these places, this was my first visit. After we parked and began to walk towards the water, I said, *"Lord, if you want to show me something this luxurious, then yes, I want a shore home as nice as the ones I see here."* Could it be possible that Holy Father wanted me to have a beautiful shore front property sooner than later? Because He and I had had this conversation years back. This place jolted that memory. I may have forgotten, but He did not forget. This was an *I can show you, better than I can tell you* moment. Could it be, that this was the way He wanted to give me something so beautiful? He had to show me the desire of His heart for me!!! Anyway, after getting our beach badges, we perched our umbrella and chairs and pulled out the chicken salad sandwiches I had made. After a while, I noticed people struggling to walk in the sand, and immediately, *a divine idea* came to me. I envisioned a solution that could possibly help lessen difficulty walking in sand. I contacted a graphic artist to draw the idea, and while speaking with someone, she suggested I contact an Invention organization, a company structured to help inventors with ideas. Believe it or not, when I reached out to them, the counselor assigned to me had already spoken to me regarding a previous project I had inquired about in 2018. But this idea, during my visit to the Belmar beach, seemed more feasible to execute!

In 2006 I purchased a used car (2002), by 2019, the engine had almost 400,000 miles on it, a good car, but it was surely falling apart. The re-inspection expired June 30th, so by September, I had been driving around for about 2.5 months with a failed sticker, a sure violation to get pulled over and fined. I generally keep things like this private, but during corporate intercessory prayer one evening, I mentioned the perils of having an automobile that old and my need for another car—which included a car payment. A sister heard about my circumstance and offered to pay for the repair, it was in the hundreds. I was able to get the repair to be able to pass the inspection; however, there remained engine challenges that could not be addressed at the time. In the interim believers prayed for me to get another car.

September 7th – prophesy: *"God says, 'even I, in this season, I AM causing you, even in your pondering, to be ushered into higher levels of responsibility, responsibility regarding your mantel, and that mantel's directives,' and what's required, says the Spirit of the living GOD. I show you certain things, but even in showing you, I will cause you in this season to act upon it and to move swiftly, or more swiftly. See, sometimes when you're in the spirit, you can move as fast as you want to or as slow. The cadence of your life has caused things to come together. In this season, I'm causing a swiftness to come upon you, and I'm causing things to catch up, because what you thought was lost in other years, I'm going to accelerate, but I need you to be positioned to receive these things quickly."*

I knew the prophecy was true because I had experienced the effortlessness of receiving the substitute teaching certification, the mantels of responsibility were changing (ministry), and I moved with a quickness to start the legal process to create and patent the invention idea that came to me at Belmar beach.

October 4th – after walking the perimeter of the sanctuary, praying, and speaking in my heavenly language, I was asked to be a second person to tag and lead in prayer, ooh! The main theme of the prayer was trusting in GOD. When the speaker came out to teach, the first phrase and topic of his presentation was *'trusting in GOD.'*

October 4th – prophesy: *I see you on the wall for somebody, I see you praying for somebody, I don't know if it's a family member or who it is, but I feel you are praying for somebody. Can I lay hands on you? "Father GOD, I thank you for this awesome intercessor, this awesome woman of GOD. When I say intercessor, I mean you're interceding for other people. I thank you that she can get a prayer through. If someone needs something, you can get a prayer through. It's like you*

23

have a unique relationship with GOD, it's like GOD is really your Father, and you're His daughter. The way you talk to GOD, the way you minister to GOD, He said you minister to Him. I don't know if you sing to Him, or what you do, but you do something that pleases His heart, when you are by yourself, or even when you are around people you bless Him, you do something that pleases His heart. But I see whoever it is in your family that you are on the wall for, I come in agreement with your prayers and decrees over this person, because I feel like it's a male. I come in agreement with it, with what you're saying in the name of Jesus, does that make sense to you? Yes! I come in agreement with you, who you're praying for, and it's going to be well. I see you like a nurse, like somebody that really, really helps people and does things for people, and you kind of put yourself to the side until you help them out, 'girl, don't worry about me, I got you.' That's why GOD loves you so much, and He really trusts you with His people. And I see Him trusting you more and more with His people in this season, because if you hadn't done or are not doing anything that's helping people, you are not in the right position, because you're supposed to be doing that. That's your whole life, blessing other people and helping them. I speak strength to you woman of GOD in the name of Jesus to keep doing what you're doing, what you're called to do. I speak blessings to come upon you from the top of your head to the soles of your feet. I speak and declare… the peace and glory and light of GOD is all over you. 'I receive it!'

Reports of a deadly disease began to surface and was spreading throughout China.

December 16th – I was walking down the hall, a brother from the *Prayer Ministry* said to me, "did you get your car yet?" I said, "no." In a stern voice, he said, "why, not?" The next morning, I was awakened *early*, it was about 4 AM, it was dark. So, I began to pray. At the end of prayer, unexpectedly I began to look online for a car. I happened upon a silver foreign luxury car that was so completely off my radar. I didn't pray for this car, but I believe it was what the *Spirit of God* led me to. I even questioned was something like this really for me? By the end of the day,

Tuesday, I was driving the car! I must say, it was one of the easiest large purchases I have ever made.

December 21st – prophesy! *In the upcoming new year, GOD is going to take care of debt(s). Write a list of the debt you currently have, be specific and include exact amounts…* I began to make a list: Auto Loan, Credit card(s), Credit Union, Goodyear, Neiman Marcus, and a student loan.

Life and death are in the power of the tongue, I can open or close doors for what I want by what I say. Circumstances come that can cause me to say things, but I need to be careful about what comes out of my mouth. I'm the one! I cannot allow circumstances to cause me to say things that are counterproductive.

A New Year, 2020!

January 2nd - for approximately twenty-one days, I began the new year substituting full-time at a middle school, then I switched over to the High School in the same county. News outlets began reporting that the Corona virus, COVID-19 had reached the United States.

February. I received a tip to begin making purchases for paper goods, bottled water and canned goods. So, I began to do just that, stock up on some things necessary for everyday survival.

Whispers!!!

March 2020. I continued substitute teaching, and I overheard talk from other teachers that public education institutions in NJ were closing rapidly because of an international and national virus, called COVID-19. Teachers were trying to remain hopeful.

On Monday, March 14th, I received an *electronic notice* that I was removed from the substitute schedule. I looked at the agency's reporting portal, in addition an announcement came from the Governor confirming mandated closings. There were hopes that schools could re-open after Easter, then maybe Memorial Day, but no. The 2019-20 academic year did not resume.

Prophesy comes to pass... as of December 21, 2019, there were six creditors. Of the six (6) creditors, all but two were paid in full by June 2020; another one was paid in full in the Spring of 2021.

Prophesy – *'angels assigned and standing guard, corporate prayer Chayil women, release upon them now GOD, a prophet's reward. In the mighty, matchless name of Jesus, do it now Father, we thank you for it, for fresh and new, and taking out everything that is not like YOU! Cheryl, I saw keys in your hands, He said these keys represent new access to new dimensions of creativity. Yes, yes, yes! There is a new chamber that just opened before you and the heavens are opened over you, Cheryl. Yes, yes, yes! I see pillows with gold tassels hanging, it is really prestigious, multiples are coming, with it are new and revised instructions. GOD is going to make a new and improved revision. The royalties coming out of it, good GOD Almighty, the level of creativity and excellence. New dreams and visions, He's getting ready to unclog demonic hairs from people and talk. He is like a liquid Drano. Royalties are coming from the throne room directly to you, one is a scroll, it's going to flow from one thing to the next, to the next, to the next. Get ready!!!*

December 21st – what is happening? This year has been the most amazing time of my life... I do not understand....

Cheryl Lavell McLeod

MIRACLES IN
PERSEVERANCE

First, I will give you a short background history of who I am and how I have persevered through the COVID-19 epidemic. I am a firm believer of the gospel of Jesus Christ. However, not to negate my faith or belief in Jesus being my healer and miracle worker, for the past several years, because of a bad car accident (which is another story all on its own), I have been suffering severe spinal and nerve pain issues, amongst other medical conditions that had been diagnosed by a medical specialist. And because of these issues, I was placed on Social Security Disability benefits. Now, anyone having any knowledge of SSD knows that the monthly payments given only allows a person to live on a low-income status. And having worked full time all my life up until the car accident, I was used to making quite a substantial yearly income.

All that has now changed. Okay, now that we are just a little caught up with my background, let's move forward. In August 2018, eight months prior to the COVID-19 Epidemic, I took on a part-time job as a caregiver. I had to take on this extra work because apparently, I had more bills than monthly earned income. My caregiving position was working out quite well for me financially. It was also very gratifying to help care for the elderly and others who had more crippling disabilities than I had. I enjoyed caring, sharing, walking, talking, listening, reading, ministering, praying, and showing love to these people with whom the Lord had allowed to be put into my care. Although I loved and enjoyed what I was doing, it became taxing on my body.

My spinal and nerve condition began to worsen. I aggravated the radiculopathy in my neck and lower lumbar. I also developed a pinched nerve in my neck and severe carpal tunnel syndrome in both my left and right hand.

If that wasn't bad enough, the diabetes I was diagnosed with (harmful and devastating), caused trigger fingers in both my hands. Trigger finger is a condition in which a finger gets stuck or locks in a bent position and then must be manually snapped straight. This was and is a very painful condition. Trigger occurs when the tendons in the affected finger or fingers become inflamed. On November 8, 2019, I had to undergo carpal tunnel surgery on my left hand and trigger finger release surgery on my left thumb and index finger. I was out of work for about three to four weeks. My doctor scheduled my next surgery for my right hand and right index finger for March 2020.

Unfortunately, that surgery had to be canceled because COVID-19 had struck the nation. It was not business as usual for anyone anywhere, in or out of the country. All or most non-essential businesses came to a close. People all over were getting sick with COVID-19, many, in the thousands, eventually dying. It was almost like experiencing a science fiction movie playing out in real life. There were a few close friends who had contracted the virus, a couple of them died. But I thank God that the majority of those I knew, family and friends included, survived because of the fervent effectual prayers of the righteous availed to the glory of God! We were forced to wear masks and use sanitizer before and after washing our hands on and off the job (at home, shopping in stores, outside etc.). We were overly cautious of whatever we touched and when around others. While many people were terrified and, in a frenzy, those of us in our church community remained calm and at peace because we knew that despite all the sickness, deaths and mayhem that was happening around us, God was still in control. He was the one giving us peace in the midst of the storm, giving His angels charge over us and our families, leaders, and communities. Ps. 91:5-11. His word says "We shall not be afraid for the terror by night nor the arrow that flieth by day.

Nor for the pestilence (Merriam-Webster definition: a contagious or infectious epidemic disease that is virulent; a disease or poison; extremely severe or widespread; or an evil influence or deliverer that walks in darkness). Therefore, with the support of God and through fasting and praying with my community prayer group, I held on strong. Most of my prayer and bible study time was on zoom with my prayer partners during this devastating epidemic. We were each other's support team. I don't know what I would have done if I didn't have a community of prayer partners. I continued working as a caregiver through the pandemic because I was working hard to pay off my lemon of a car. It was a 2006 Buick Lacrosse. Between the high maintenance upkeep, the monthly car payments, and the two rent payments (one apartment and the other was a three-bedroom storage), I was barely making ends meet. I was exhausted and living with insufferable silent pain in my body. After a while, it started getting very hard to get out of bed. Whenever I'd be lying down and trying to stand up to go to the bathroom, the pain in my lower back and extremities would be so intensely painful that it caused incontinence and I wouldn't make it to the bathroom. There have been several instances when I would wake up in bed soiled because of the severity of the spinal pain, I wouldn't feel my bladder or my bowels releasing until it was too late. This happened whether it was morning, afternoon, or the middle of the night. I started to become depressed and very embarrassed about what I was going through in my body. I still pushed myself through this pain, which increased even more as time went on, but I kept on working to pay my bills and pay off my car. I had also been diagnosed with Diabetes Mellitus and Asthma some years before, it put me at a very high risk for contracting the COVID-19 Virus. Praise Jesus, He continued to protect and keep me while I worked. I asked myself how long I could keep taking a risk with my health and life?

On June 23, 2020, I had to have carpal tunnel surgery on my right hand. While I was home convalescing, at around 4:30 PM, a woman had fallen asleep while driving and crashed right into my parked car. My car was completely totaled. I happened to have my blinds up while watching television in bed and I witnessed the whole thing. I was in total shock and disbelief that this had happened. I slowly and carefully climbed out of my bed, put on my pants and shoes, and went to make sure everyone was alright. Once I was sure no one was hurt, including the person who had run into my car, then I became upset and wanted an answer about what had just happened. I found out from the woman driver that she had fallen asleep while on her way to pick up her brother, who by the way, lived almost two buildings away from me on the opposite side of the street. Then to my further disbelief, this same woman confessed that this was her second time falling asleep at the wheel. Well, when she told me this, I began to give her a sharp reprimand. I told her she could have taken someone's life and that she needs to see a doctor about her condition. She had totaled two cars that day, mine, and another neighbors. My car was hit so hard that it was pushed into the back of my other neighbor's car. We were just grateful that this woman didn't take a life, including her own. After putting almost $9,000 into that car, I only got back $2,400 after paying off the $1,600 that was owed. I was very angry and dismayed. After working all that time to fix up and pay off the car, I barely got enough money back to buy another one. Although I did try. When my hand began to heal up some, a neighbor friend of mine started helping me search for another used car. The search went on for a few months to no avail. Finally, I gave up and started using money I had gotten from the insurance to pay my bills. I was not getting paid to be on medical leave each time I had a surgery. Because I was a part-time worker, I did not get any benefits. So, there I was, without transportation, and without a way to go back to work. You must have a vehicle to work as a caregiver, you cannot work or be hired without one.

I didn't want to tell my job that I no longer had a car, so I said nothing. When I did not return to work after several weeks of medical leave, I was terminated. When they asked my reason for not returning, I told them it was because of diabetes and asthma, which put me at risk for contracting COVID-19. It really was the truth, although, I did hold back the fact that I no longer had transportation. After a while, I was kind of relieved that I did not go back to work. I did still have my SSD benefit to help pay my rent, storage, and a little food. Hey, I was still grateful to God for a roof over my head, a few bills paid, and food. Nonetheless, a month or two after my hand had healed from surgery, I had to have a trigger finger release surgery on my right index finger. Man, I was starting to feel like Ms. Frankenstein. Then, after a visit to my spine specialist/surgeon, he decided to schedule me an L4-S1 laminectomy, and an L4-L5 posterior spinal fusion because of all the pain and trauma I was suffering in my lower back and extremities. The surgery was scheduled for July 6, 2020. Mind you, he did not take into consideration that I was still just recovering from surgery on my right hand, and that I didn't really have anyone living with me to care for me and my chihuahua. So, I pushed the date back to

October 19, 2020. Now, although I had a community of prayer partners that kept me encouraged, there were times when I found myself feeling discouraged, depressed, and sometimes alone. And even though I knew God was with me, despite my faith, I was becoming more depressed and anxious about my situation. Don't get me wrong, I prayed God's word over my life situations, and I believed and still believe that God had already healed me, and He was working things out for my good. I guess I was just becoming weary of waiting on the manifestation of His healing and promises. Anyhow, I had already been seeing a counselor on a regular basis for about a year.

I was told that I had severe depression and anxiety. I knew I felt depression and anxiety try to overtake me every now and again, but I did not realize it was to that extent.

You could never look at me and tell that I was depressed, because it never showed on my face or countenance. I would always have a smile on my face if I was greeting someone, or I would be laughing with the neighbors or watching the kiddos play with my dog. I guess, deep down inside I was unhappy with myself, my life, health, and financial situation. I was still attending bible study and prayer on Zoom on a regular monthly and bi-weekly basis. Besides God's grace and mercy, I really believe this is what kept me structured and focused throughout the whole pandemic crisis and my health ordeal.

Well, just when I thought it couldn't get any worse, I received letters from the Social Security Administration stating that they had decided to end my disability and that I was not entitled to SSD payments, which supposedly went into effect July 2019. According to them, my disability ends if my work activity shows my ability to do substantial work. Now, I have never stopped being under the care of my primary care, orthopedic specialists, and spine & pain management physicians.

Had they researched or asked for my current records, they would have known that I still had a disability, although I tried my best to fake the funk and work, instead of trusting God to provide as He always has done. But that is neither here nor there, I had thirty days before my disability ended. I contacted someone from the Social Security Administration office for an appeal. They mailed me at least three to four packets of forms to fill out. There was a total of 103 forms altogether, and of course they gave me a short deadline to get it back to their office. I tried to explain that I had recently had surgery on my right hand (primary hand), and it would be difficult to write, let alone get it done on time. It did not seem to matter to them. As very painful as it was, I did my best to get as many forms completed as possible and mailed out. By that next week, I received another letter from the Social Security Administration, stating this, "Because we did not stop your checks until December 2020, and you were paid $24,576.00".

We were still in December though! If I wasn't in panic mode the first time, I surely was right now! All I could do was yell aloud "HELLO!", If I am unable to work physically and you guys are terminating my benefits, where and how on earth, am I supposed to come up with that type of money? Surely these people have lost their mind! I was thinking I should maybe let them borrow my therapist. Thank God I still had some humor in me. Sometimes, you have to laugh to keep from crying. The year before, prior to COVID-19, on or around tax season, the IRS had sent me a letter stating that I owed $43,000 for back tax and late filing. I won't lie, my heart did skip a couple of beats, but I kept my cool. I knew I didn't have that money to pay back, but I also knew that they would work with me. And then Covid hit. So, fast forwarding back to the SSD benefit termination, when December 1, 2020, came, I noticed that my SSD benefits did not get deposited in my account. My benefits were indeed terminated. That meant, no rent or any bills for that matter were going to get paid unless the Lord sent me a financial miracle. I called on the aid of my prayer partners. We fasted and touched and agreed on the matter at hand along with other prayer requests. On Wednesday, December 2, 2020, I contacted a disability legal aid.

She met and consulted with me outside my apartment that very next day. She advised me to continue filling out any and all forms the SSA sends out to me, and then she would pick them up from me and get them to their office. And she did just that. She was very thorough and diligent. While my legal aid was working behind the scenes, kind of like the Lord, I contacted my apartment office manager and informed her of my situation. She was very helpful in assisting me with the rental assistance application. She told me not to worry if I didn't hear back from them right away and that it may take a while, but not to panic. The Lord had indeed given me favor with this woman. Meanwhile, I kept nagging my legal aid. She assured me that she would get SSA to send out emergency pay to me.

I kept praying and believing in God for the miracle of my benefits being reinstated and the overpayment of $24,576 waived. Weeks went by, and I hadn't heard anything back from the SSA. According to my legal aid, my case was still in the determination phase. By January 1, 2021, I still had not received any benefit pay. But God came through by way of my prayer community team. Each of the nine people on our team was simultaneously sending cash via a cash app. Some brought over needed essentials that I couldn't go out and buy either because of lack of car or funds. They were dropping off cases of water, juices, paper products, cleaning products and even food. When I say that God had supplied all of my needs, He truly did, through His children. Not only did He use the beautiful team of women in my prayer group, but He also used some of my neighbors who knew nothing about what I was going through. Some happened to be going to the grocery store or the food bank and they would call to ask if I wanted to come along, and of course I went. Then, when I told them that they were being a blessing to me unaware, they insisted that I call on them whenever I needed a ride or anything else. Even now, thinking about it as I write, all I can say is to God be the glory!! Even in the midst of all I was going through, He was with me. By the end of January, I still had not received any benefits. This continued well into May or June. By then I had applied for general assistance and Snap food benefits.

However, I only received $79 a month from general assistance. Actually, the first check was only $64.00. I could not pay rent with that but still, I was humble and grateful for the little I was receiving. It was a good thing that I had still had a little money left in my secret stash to get me by, but soon that too was diminished. Sometime around the middle or end of June 2021, the property manager called me to say that I had finally been approved for the rental assistance and that they were going to pay my back rent from December 2020, up to July 2021. How great a blessing and miracle was that? I was so relieved and happy.

I couldn't wait to tell my testimony to my prayer community, because I knew this would give them hope and encouragement to know that prayer changes things and God is still in control.

Now, it is November 2021, and I am still currently waiting for the Social Security Administration to determine whether or not they are going to reinstate my case. Each month since September 2021, my legal aid attorney has had to put in a request for them to give me emergency funds.

My appeal is still ongoing. But am I worried? Nope! Am I still suffering from severe disabling pain? Yes! But guess what? God has me covered!!

Theresa Menefee

WEATHERED
THE STORM

I was so determined to start my newly formed transportation company. I was so excited to meet and transport people with transportation needs to their appointments. Although I did not have my first client, you could not tell me I was not ready for business.

I planned to start contacting nursing facilities, residential facilities, and social services agencies throughout my county to inform them Community Links Transportation Services, LLC was in business!

Again, I was so excited my long-awaited dream since 2018 was becoming my reality. I can remember staying up late and waking up early to create forms, research other transportation companies, and to create a catchy sales pitch. I made checklists for days ahead and made sure I worked hard to accomplish them, and I refused to let anything stop me.

On March 3, 2020, I signed my lease for the lower-level office space. I was so excited to just hold the pen to sign the lease. Once I received my key, I began decorating my new space. I called my sister as I began hanging up pictures to tell her the good news, we both began praising God. I was singing, and she was dancing, Brandy was so encouraged she soon created a natural beauty line.

After the first week, I met some of the other business owners in the office building. Although I was excited, my husband was not. He constantly reminded me of how he did not feel as though now was a good time to get the office space. He was concerned about the cost of the office space and the other overheads that came with running a transportation business. He complained, "you just started, and you have no clients, how are you going to pay your rent next month?" However, with the lease signed there was no turning back. I would just say, with laughter, "you are such a hater, relax! I got this!"

I had already told my family members and friends about my new endeavors. I had even planned to hire some of them once Community Links Transportation Services was established.

I began going to the office to make phone calls and to network with the other business owners to determine if I could assist their clients with their transportation needs. Though I was a stay-at-home mom with two kids I was homeschooling, I brought them to the office as well. I planned to enroll them in a learning center once I received my first contract.

I was determined to sign at least one contract. I remember contacting an Assisted Living Facility with the hopes to sign that first contract. As I began to tell her about my transportation services, she seemed more interested when I told her the cost. To my surprise, she asked me to mail her my policy with my price included. She stated she planned to speak with her supervisor as soon as he was out of his meeting. She sounded very excited and told me this pay rate was the best rate she had seen from any transportation company.

It wasn't until after I sent her my rates and she called me back that I realized I quoted her the wrong amount by several dollars. I then realized why she had wanted my payment scale in writing. After that phone call, I realized I was moving too fast, and I had to slow down if I wanted to receive the proper contracts.

It was three weeks later my Pastor, Pastor James, sent a group text message to the church members stating we needed to begin storing up dry goods and canned goods. He said there were going to be some changes that would be taking effect, and to be prepared by storing up. I remember wondering what was going on, and though I was puzzled, I did as he instructed. I bought dry beans and pasta and beans from Dollar Tree, rice, water, and canned chicken from Sam's Club, and canned goods from my local grocery store.

Within a few weeks, I'd begun hearing about the coronavirus and how it was affecting so many people's lives, to the point of death. The news stations constantly reported of how people were dying, it was being reported in record-breaking numbers. I remember asking myself how I could have missed this, despite there being no signs of this instant virus. I had always tried to be prepared for things to come, but this time I was not.

There was a new mandate requiring all residents to maintain a six feet distance from others, and to wear a face mask. A mask, I thought, what is happening to the world? And how did it change so quickly?

After Pastor James told us about storing up, I found myself at the grocery store every week, if not twice a week. At Sam's Club, I often noticed the line to enter the store appeared longer and longer each time I went. It was as if everyone had received the same text from Pastor James! I remember times when I went to the store early so that I could be in the first few to enter, however, there was still a long line and I had to stand in line in the cold, wearing my face mask (a mask that would let you know when your breath needed to be refreshed!) to enter the store to purchase food.

I thought this was all too much for me, standing in line for food, wearing a face mask, sanitizing my hands so many times throughout the day, and standing six feet away from others. However, I knew I had to quickly adapt if I wanted to purchase food and even go out in public. Trying to remain positive, I often told myself this was not going to always be like this, and to just relax, due to sometimes feeling overwhelmed.

At times, all I could think about was my business and how I was not prepared for the coronavirus. I did not know if the people I would be transporting to their appointments would have the virus and if I would contract it while transporting them to their appointments. I thought, I have three small children, and I'm not sure a mask would save me or them from becoming sick. Trying to block out the possibility of closing my business was hard for me to bear. However, two months after signing my lease I had to terminate it. Brokenhearted and disappointed, I met with the leasing agent to return him the key to my office space.

I never got my first client, never had a chance to smile at them as I walked them back to their front door, or even the chance to say thank you for using our transportation services, and that I hoped we exceeded their expectations. Nothing. As I drove home, I tried my best to understand how something such as a virus could cause so many to go out of business, people to lose their jobs, cause so many deaths, and so much fear.

As much as I had tried not to let anything stop me from operating my business, the coronavirus did. Though the thought of crying and feeling like a failure crossed my mind for some strange reason, I could do neither. I began thinking about one night when after prayer, my Assistant Pastor told me not to make any moves concerning my business for there was going to be something like a storm going to happen, and God did not want me to be affected by it.

However, I did not take heed. It was at that moment I realized that my disobedience was the real reason I had to close my business, not the coronavirus. Once home, I saw my husband smiling, waiting to say his favorite words. I just rolled my eyes at him. As I began warming a bagel, a bagel I stood in line for what seemed to be hours to purchase at the grocery store, I sat down to turn on the television. It seemed all channels were only showing the data of the high number and location of the newly infected people with the coronavirus. It seemed like this news story was on every television station, even on shows that were not news stations, showing the high case numbers captioned at the bottom of the screen. And though I was disappointed, I thanked God in my head that I had closed my transportation business. And I say in my head I thanked Jesus, because that husband of mine was still looking at me smiling and waiting to say his favorite words, "I told you so."

I often heard from God, as He told me of different places to purchase food. He began telling me to purchase storage bins to store the dry and canned food. Some days I tried to push His directions to the back of my mind, not wanting to go to another store. However, I felt His tugging. I began getting up early in the morning before the grocery stores even opened. I waited in the parking lot with my list in my hand, waiting for the doors to open. I thought of how I would feel to hear my children complaining to me there was no food to eat, and that they were hungry. Between God's tugging on me and thinking of my children, I had no choice but to be obedient.

I laugh to myself sometimes, because I had even discussed with my husband of the need to purchase food. He often thought I was crazy and told me to please stop buying food, but soon he became on board and began purchasing items as well. However, after two months, he complained saying, "please don't buy another case of water, box of pasta, and no more beans, we have enough food." Though I agreed, there was no way I would stop storing food as long as he and the kids were eating what we had stored!

Though the school year was close to ending it would not be long before the schools ended their in-school service. My son would begin attending school virtually, I had the task of helping him complete assignments and turn them in on time. I was glad to be a stay-at-home mom because I love spending time with my son.

I know if I had started my transportation business, it would not be long before I would have to make some decisions of closing it, due to not being able to work. I wasn't financially ready to enroll three kids into a learning center. I was glad that my son was home with me, but at times it was overwhelming because of the sudden changes that were taking place due to the pandemic.

I felt like I was being swallowed up with the responsibility of caring for the kids and my home with no real outlet. Everything seemed to be closing down around me, my social life was becoming non-existent because I was fearful of not knowing if my friends had the virus. Just being around people sometimes made me nervous, especially if they coughed. This could not be my new normal.

In the month of June, it seemed as if the coronavirus was on a vengeance, devouring whoever was in its way. The new numbers of those testing positive had drastically increased and the number of deaths throughout the world had increased as well. The news stations continued to report the hospitalizations and those who were on ventilators, it seemed like around the clock.

As much as the world was changing as a result of the coronavirus, my life was changing also. No longer could I attend our church service or Bible Study, (services were now viewed on Zoom), I couldn't take my kids to Chuck E. Cheese (their favorite place), or even to the park, and I had soon stopped taking my children inside the stores.

We spent more time in the house, due to believing the virus was in the air, according to the news. At times, I wasn't sure if I could handle another cartoon episode of Super Why! I soon became the creative queen in the house. I gave myself the duty of finding and creating activities for my children that often made them happy.

Though it was tough God allowed me to make it through. Although the world had been greatly affected by the coronavirus and the world seemed to be at a standstill, I used this time to be still and to draw close to God. I don't know if it was too much zeal or a hunger for God, but I would wake up at 5 o'clock every morning to begin prayer at 5:30am. After washing my face and brushing my teeth, I began to pray, listening for God's voice, and reading my words as if my life depended on it.

My friends often noticed my early awakening and my conversation when they called, by saying, "you've been praying this morning again, huh?" Though I just laughed, it was as if God was taking me on a higher journey in Him. He was enlarging me while giving my life substance. I soon began praying every Thursday on the church prayer line, which I continue to do to this day.

God was establishing me. I believe that through this establishing, my family and I were able to avoid contracting the coronavirus and survive the aftermath of the virus. My husband went to work every day, and once back home, he would tell me of those from his job that had contracted the virus, and though they had it, he never contracted it.

God is truly a keeper! God instructed me to purchase several bottles of Zinc. I heard His voice, but I questioned Him, "like really, God, Zinc? What is that?" He took me to a video where a doctor suggested the same zinc to keep one's immune system built up. My thoughts of this is, always believe God, despite your earthly thinking, and be obedient, even when it doesn't make sense.

I often look back at the effect of the coronavirus on the world and on my life. And unlike some people in the world, I thank God I have not been affected as others have. My husband, who continues to work, never got sick, nor me, nor my children. He was not laid off and never missed a paycheck. We never lost our possessions waiting on the government to give us stimulus benefits. My children continued to be provided for with no concerns. None of my family members contracted the coronavirus and I have not had any friends or loved one die because of the virus.

I also have to say, there have been some other benefits for us, despite the effects of the coronavirus. In August 2020, we purchased a home, in October 2020, I wrote and self-published a book titled *Overcomer by God's Grace,* and in December 2020, I created and self-published a Workbook Journal to go with my book titled the *Overcomer by God's Grace Workbook Journal.* I have had vending opportunities that have brought in finances to support my business. I give God all the glory!

Today I can say I have weathered and continue to weather the storm of the coronavirus. I continue to stay close to God by reading his word, praying more, listening for his voice, and most of all, I have a relationship with Him.

I am no longer getting up at 5am, but I am getting up each morning to pray, listening for God's voice for instructions and strategies, and to read my Word to continue to Overcome.

Through my obedience to God, my family has never missed a meal, we have been able to live life with no constraints associated with the virus, and we continue to trust God in all things. I am still storing food, water, and supplies. I am also encouraging others to do the same, not just for themselves, but for others.

My transportation business is still not open; however, God has allowed me to revamp my business, and once instructed, I will re-open.

During this time of the coronavirus pandemic, I opened my transportation business, not realizing that there would be a pandemic. Due to my disobedience, I had opened and closed my transportation business in less than three months. Although I received a warning from God and my husband, I still did not listen, and as a result I was heartbroken and disappointed.

During the time of the virus, I also had times of feeling overwhelmed, physically and socially isolated, and put in a box. However, I still made it through the pandemic, through the Grace of God. He kept me and my family from contracting the coronavirus, we never lost anything, but we gained everything!

We purchased a home, I created and published a book and a journal, and most of all, my relationship with God was strengthened through having time to read my word, pray, spend time with God, and listen for his voice.

This is my story, my testimony, it is my prayer that you are strengthened and encouraged to know that God is a keeper, and he will keep you when in a pandemic and when not in a pandemic. He is able!

During this time, I learned to have Faith in God. Thanks to the pandemic/reset, I began spending more time with God and at that time I began to really understand that I can speak for myself and my family knowing that God has given me the power to Decree and Declare. The power of life and death is in my mouth.

Joi' Jno-Baptiste

FORGIVE & TRUST AGAIN

In February 2019, I had to gather my family and rush to North Carolina because my mother had taken ill. We piled into cars and raced to North Carolina in the dead of winter. Other family members flew in from Arizona and Antigua. When we arrived, she was already in a hospice.

I watched my mother deal with a great amount of trauma her whole life, with enormous loss and with disappointment after disappointment. I never had the chance to see her heal from them. We never talked about emotional pain, I was never taught how to navigate through trauma or distress. All I ever saw was my mom working, and she did that well.

I was raised in a strict West Indian household. What happened in our house stayed in our house, that was law. The love and the grace I have for my mother grows more now during her death, because when she was alive, I just couldn't understand some things.

When I arrived in NC, I saw a frail and bedridden woman who just in December had been feisty and full of life. She didn't want to live, and she vocalized it with no hesitation. She declined all treatment and was ready to die. No number of tears or pleading would change her mind, and here I was again facing trauma. On her deathbed, she said something that still rings in my ears, she said, "Marsha, God knows and sees all, He knows." I was very mad at her for giving up, but she was tired and heartbroken, and I wish she had had the chance to experience God's true healing power.

I went home to Boston and decided that I would not work myself to death as my mother did. I would do things my own way and on my own terms. I would not let a job rob me of my good years. I would be free and do as I please, and let God in there somewhere, He just wouldn't have full, control because in reality who gives up full control and what does that even look like? If I had to suffer like the people in the bible, I wanted no part of it. I had suffered enough, and I decided to love God just enough.

I packed up and moved myself and my young son to Dallas, Texas. It was Mother's Day weekend and early that Saturday my daughter gave birth to my youngest grandson. That was the best Mother's Day present I could have ever received, but I had no time to stay around and bask.

I had to leave because I needed to spend Mother's Day with my mom, and it was in-route to Texas. So, I drove straight to NC. When I got there, I spent the night with my mother. I honestly did not think it would be the last time I got to hug her and tell her I love her. I figured we still had time. She had already lived longer than expected and there was closure that I needed. My last memory of my mother was her saying "Marsha...Marsha I am, I am (in faint whispers) Marsha." I simply said, "it's okay and I know, I know Mom." A part of me knew that it was an attempted apology, I saw the remorse in her eyes, but I wasn't ready to accept that she might not be here, that this could possibly mean goodbye, so I told her to save that for our next conversation. I needed to cry, I needed her to tell me that she loved me, I needed an explanation as to why she couldn't love me while I was growing up. Why did she think I was worthless? This was a word that to that day still stopped me in my tracks and caused me to have anxiety. There were so many questions, and they were accompanied by pain.

I arrived in Dallas and started my new job. I loved everything about Dallas and still do. I decided that I would do it my way and prove everyone wrong, that I could make it on "my own," by myself. I didn't need anyone. After two weeks in Dallas, I received the call that my mother had transitioned.

I had never learned how to deal with trauma and grief, so I realized at that moment that I would never get the answers to all the questions I had. I thought I would be broken and hurt forever. Unloved forever. So, I did what I knew how to do, I went to North Carolina and remained "strong," even though I felt so overwhelmed and weak.

We buried my mom and when I returned, I was let go from my job. I was told the client was unhappy because I had been on my phone, and it was unprofessional. I took that blow in stride and buried yet another loss because I just had to be strong and keep it moving. In my mind I would pull through because I always pulled through, no matter the hurt, pain, or disappointments, I made sure I pulled through. I was really dying on the inside. Looking back, I can only thank God for His love, His grace, and His mercy.

I found a new job, and even though they promised me a management position, I settled into a lesser position. Shortly after, I was promoted, I had to move. At that point, I wasn't making the money I was used to making and things became difficult. I decided I was not leaving Texas come hell, or high-water, so my son and I started living out of my car. There were many nights I just sat up and cried as he slept in the back seat, and I felt abandoned by God. Just another blow, but I was used to the blows, and I would pull through. I really did not trust God; I did not trust His love for me, I did not trust or expect Him to provide or take care of Moses and me.

The circumstances in my life began to prove my belief system to be correct. I lost my job within a week of becoming homeless. My assignment had ended by this point. It was February of 2020. I thought about Boston and how I went from a job making close to six figures to now living in my car, jobless and homeless. I still refused to ask for help.

I finally gave in, and because of the pleas of my best friend and daughter, I left for NC, defeated and angry at God because He just kept taking everything from me. I was mad! However, during this time, I had a group of sisters who were praying for me and with me, and no matter how broken I was, God still held on to me, He still ministered to me and little did I know — He had a plan for me.

The pandemic hit as soon as I arrived in NC. Everything shut down and the entire world stood still. I thought about how I had just escaped being in a really bad situation with my son, because we had nowhere to go. I was bitter and mad, and unable to grieve.

I stayed in NC from February until June, and during that time I was able to spend quality time with my grandchildren. However, there was a part of me that was so empty, so broken, so afraid and so angry. I decided to move back to Boston in June 2020. What I said I would never do; I was now doing. I was going back to Boston, angry, afraid, broken and hurt. It had been an entire year since my mom had passed and I was still just coping with it, not grieving, not growing, just barley existing. I thank God for the people he had in place to love me; childhood friends, my nieces, they played a huge part in my healing process.

I arrived in Boston, broke in more ways than one. I was broken spiritually, emotionally, and mentally, and I was broke financially. I felt hopeless, lost, and ashamed. At this point I had no one to trust but God, and He started to provide for me in ways I didn't think He would. I was jobless, homeless and yet I was provided for and flourishing. I thought, "oh, maybe God does like me, maybe He does care."

Just when I felt like I could begin to breathe, my older sister suddenly transitioned. I was at a loss for words and just could not believe that I had to endure yet another blow, another loss. By this point I had experienced the deaths of four people I loved, and I was utterly broken the night before my sister passed, I laid in bed half sleep, and all of a sudden, I felt God pushing me to get up and go and see her. I thought to myself, "I will go tomorrow," but I could not shake the feeling that I needed to see her. I went to my niece's house and spent some time with her. I had decided to take care of her because I didn't get to be with my mom and care for her. My biggest regret is not praying for her when I felt led to.

My sister transitioned that night. I couldn't understand why God would take her. I didn't have enough time with her. After her heart attack, I told myself I would make sure to be present for her and to love her, and that chance was ripped away from me. I felt so numb. God was orchestrating my steps and ultimately my healing.

If I had not been forced from Dallas, I would not have been able to see and spend time with my sister before she passed. I wouldn't have been in the right place to be there for my nieces, and that alone would have buried me in grief. I was battling anxiety, depression, and grief. I could not understand why I had to deal with and face so much hurt and trauma.

My entire life had been full of trauma from being gang raped as a teenager, mental and physical abuse as a child, molestation, abandonment, being robbed at gun point and almost killed, and battling suicidal thoughts throughout my entire life, I was at a point where I just could not go on anymore. Some days, I couldn't tell my left from my right, and even though people were all around me, no one picked up on the state I was in other than my best friend. I remember her telling me "Marsha, you have to get back in that space where you let God have control, you cannot do it alone." I didn't realize that I was going off of my own strength, I had gotten so used to just doing it myself that I didn't realize I had excluded God from leading, providing and simply loving me. I believed God for everybody else, I prayed for everyone else, but when it came to myself, I felt that God wouldn't, and I didn't deserve for Him to, love me, provide for me, and heal me. I was too broken to be fixed. I wasn't enough. I was worthless and unlovable.

This is who I thought I was. I could not wrap my mind around God truly loving me because it was imbedded in me at an early age that I was worthless and would never amount to be anything, that I was a useless dog. These are the words that the enemy had continually reminded me of throughout my life and sadly I believed them.

The back-to-back trauma and loss had gripped me to my soul's core. I had been in two failed relationships between 2016 and 2020 that rocked me and caused me to doubt myself and God's love even more. Everything was failing, my trust in God was basically nonexistent. However, I never stopped believing He was God, I just believed He wasn't for me, that He wouldn't rescue me, that He could not possibly love me because I was unlovable. Fear engulfed me, but I was used to fear, it had been a part of my life since childhood and in some ways, I found it comforting because I could fall back on it, fear would always catch me. The fear of failing, fear of doing good, fear of dying, fear of living, I was just a mess mentally, and I decided I would hide.

I had been hiding for so long that I was comfortable in my place of darkness. I knew all along that God had gifted me, that He was calling me, but the traumas I had experienced left me delusional and incoherent to God, His will, and His Word, so I decided I would do absolutely nothing. I would do enough, what I thought was enough, to just get by, to just be present, to just show I loved God and my family, but inside I was numb and on the verge of dying. There was a part of me that was pushing and fighting, but I was trapped by depression, anxiety, and most of all, fear.

I had reached a breaking point. I was exhausted. I didn't even have the strength to cry out to God. Some days I just sat in the living room on the couch and stared at the walls. I had learned how to put up a good front around others but at home I was just there. I was always yelling at my son, and I barely talked to anyone, I just wanted to be left alone. Inside I was crying out for help, I thought my cries were not heard.

God heard me. He saw me, my heart, I don't know how, but even when I was completely silent and nonverbal, He heard me. I remember calling Dr. Brown and just talking to her. We always talked, so it was nothing out of the ordinary. However, during this conversation she invited me to just listen in on prayer and to participate in The Prophetic Institute. I was leary, I didn't want to hear prophecy, didn't want to hear what God had to say, didn't want to be bothered, and I was just very annoyed. I reluctantly joined. Trust me when I say I went in with my guard up. I had already shot down every prayer and any word that I would hear, I had given up on being free.

During one of the sessions, the guest Pastor began to talk about trauma, and I sat there thinking, "that's all I know." I began questioning God immediately, "How do I get past all this trauma? How do I heal? Why won't You heal me? The floor was open for questions, and I simply asked, "Why do I feel like I keep returning to this place of trauma?" It was during this encounter when I learned how to deal with my trauma head on, I learned what the real purpose of trauma was and how it was meant to keep me from ever trusting God. It had served its purpose because I refused to trust God. I loved God, but I told myself I would never trust Him, and I grouped Him in with everyone who had hurt me, left me, abandoned me, and failed me.

What had taken me half of my life to deal with, was now being dealt with in the midst of isolation. I was alone with my thoughts, restricted by a pandemic. I had time, opportunity, and space to deal with my heart's issues, and God wasted no time on tuning me up. I look back now and realize he had to force me to this space because I busied myself with the concerns and affairs of everyone else. I was too preoccupied, too involved, and off focus, God could not reach me. If I didn't like something I left. If I didn't want to deal with people, I left. The truth is, I had been running from myself, from the deep-rooted pain, but I didn't have anywhere else left to run I had to be still. It was in the quiet, the darkness of isolation, the middle of a pandemic, when people were losing their lives, their hopes, when others were losing the battle to depression that God breathed new life into me and spoke life to my dry bones.

I remember while praying I heard The Lord say to me "So what do you have to blame now? Who do you have to blame now? What is your excuse now? She is gone and you will never get an explanation nor an apology, so what will you choose now?" I was appalled, and angry that He would question me during what I was enduring, but God in His infinite wisdom said "if you let me, I will give you life and an abundant life, life beyond the hurt and pan, life beyond the disappointments, if you choose to let me. This was the intimacy I needed, this was a relationship and not religion. This was God taking time out to reach me and pursue me. I realized it was my choice. My choice to forgive, my choice to live and to trust. My choice to be loved or my choice to die. So, I decided to face my fears head on. I decided to do the work and I decided to yield and surrender. I look back at all the years of hurt and depression and all the years of refusing to surrender, how those years almost ate me alive and in the matter of a few months, how God had begun to chip away at the brick enclosure around my heart. That enclosure made me miss out on so many opportunities, but God began to demonstrate how He would restore me, mind, body, and soul.

Trusting still did not come easy and there were times when I felt as if I were crazy. I had to realize that God watches over His Word and that His word would accomplish what He sent it to do. One of my greatest breakthroughs came when I faced the fact that my mother had been traumatized herself and did not know how to deal with all the neglect and hurt, she had dealt with, so she worked herself to death. I had to face the fact that she didn't have the ability to be supportive or show me love as a child and as I grew. Because she was never healed, she was unable to give me that love as I became an adult, but I did know that she loved me. I learned to look past the abuse and extend grace to my mother. It was a different level of forgiveness and that forgiveness freed me in so many areas where I had locked the door to keep others out, to keep God out.

Allowing God access to every part of you can be scary, but it is so therapeutic, to put it mildly. I had to really understand what trusting Him was. He says that His plans for you are to prosper and not harm you, to give you hope and a future. I had lost hope and here was God showing me and telling me He wanted to give *me* hope. I had walked around for years consumed by suicidal thoughts, battling demons and depression, feeling unloved and unworthy, even when I had heard the truth, even when I had ministered this truth to everyone else. I was surrounded by so many people, yet no one saw past the facade. I was unable to accept love because of trauma. "I had to fight all my life," (y'all know the line) and I was tired of fighting. In these moments, the only thing that kept me from ending my life was the fear of not knowing what would happen to my son and what would happen to my grandchildren.

When I realized trauma was a tool of the enemy to distance me from God and to make me believe that He could not possibly love me or want me, I felt like I had the big joker and was about to run a Boston on that fool. All the spades' players should be able to understand, it was like, huh, wait, what? I woke up. I woke up grateful, my eyes were open, and I could see, my ears were open, and I could hear, my strength was restored, and I wasn't weak or feeble. Most of all, I was willing to yield and surrender in areas I never thought I would give to God, and that was another battle all in itself. I had to relearn how to walk (in God). I am grateful for muscle memory because it wasn't too long, and I was back in the race. God reminded me that the race wasn't given to the fastest or the strongest, but to the one who would endure. God's Word was once again alive in me and to me. With that, I encourage you to press toward the mark of the high calling. Forget those things behind and press on!

Marsha Joseph

IN PURSUIT OF GOD

Psalms 118: 24-29 The Lord has done it this very day; let us rejoice today and be glad.

Lord, save us! Lord, grant us success! Blessed Is he who comes in the name of the Lord.

From the house of The Lord, we bless you. The Lord is God, and He has made his light shine on us. With boughs in hand, join in the festival procession. Up the horns of the altar. You are my God, and I will praise you; You are my God, I will exalt you. Give thanks to the Lord, for he is good; His Love endures forever.

Back to the Basics — putting him first. Making God the head of my life for real again. Not material things, or ambitions, or what I drive, but what is driving me. Why was I driven to accept him in my life?

I can remember accepting Christ as my personal Lord and savior when I was 19 years old, almost 20. I was involved with this young man who barely knew how to love himself, so he could not have known how to love another. I felt so alone. My family was too busy to notice I needed a hand in life. In short, they didn't have what I needed, but Jesus knew all about it. So, I was adopted by another community of women, my village. The women in the house on Devon Street in Dorchester, MA became my village. My children and I were hanging out with them all the time. In doing so, I met this incredible young lady by the name of Felicia. The second time we met she was singing from her bed, a song by Anita Baker and The Winans song, *Ain't no need to worry what the night is gonna bring, it'll be all over in the morning.* She was in bed, stricken by this condition called sciatica. I didn't know what it was, all I knew was that she had trouble walking. She had a walker cane like old people use, as I stated earlier in my writing a lot of reasons why Christ is my personal LORD AND SAVIOR.

Felicia's cousin Jay was, tragically, lost in a motorcycle accident, so family members came to Boston MA for the burial. They were sitting around reflecting on Jay's life. Then Felicia's Aunt Jeanette asked me a question, "are you saved? Do you know Jesus as your personal Lord and savior, that he died on the cross for your sins and the sins of the world?" I answered, "no I do not know Jesus Christ as my personal Lord and savior." We said the sinner's prayer and I asked him to come into my heart.

Romans 10: 10-13. *For with the heart, man believeth unto righteousness; and with the mouth, confession is made unto salvation. For the scripture saith whosoever believeth in him shall not be ashamed. For there is no difference between the Jew and the Greek: for the same Lord overall is rich unto all that He calls upon the Hill. 13. For whosoever shall call upon the name of the Lord shall be saved.* I've said the sinners' prayer from that day until now. I am saved by His grace.

Fast-forward to the present time, 2021. All of these events took place globally. I wondered, was I praying in vain? I'm praying for stuff, and I forgot the true purpose of the Gospel of Jesus Christ. We had Mass shootings, on 9/11, one of the planes was hijacked from MA, a child in Massachusetts was in a family day care and somehow made it up to the roof, fell off, and died. My spirit was beginning to question what I was praying for. I sat before GOD in silence because my heart was broken, even before coming into the new year saying I WILL never ask the Lord when or how.

Mathew 6:24-27 *No one can serve two masters: either he will hate the one and love the other, or he will be devoted to the one and despise the other. You cannot serve both God and money. Therefore, I tell you, do not worry about your life, what you will eat or drink, or about your body, what you will wear. Is not life more than food and the body more than clothes? Who of you, by worrying, can add a single hour to life?* I've been through a lot of things in my life, BUT God is my Battle Axe, my very present help in times of trouble, so I don't worry. I repented because I started to count on my resources. Foolishly, I was under the impression that these things were obtained with my own strength.

Psalm 75:6- *For Promotion cometh neither from the east nor from the west nor from the south.* According to the book of Psalms, here we are again, needing a hedge of protection like never before. Nothing was the same, everything changed.

With boughs in hand, join in the festal procession up to the horns of the altar. You are my God, and I will give you thanks; you are my God and I will exalt you. Give thanks to the Lord, for he is good; his love endures forever. Psalms 118:24-29NIV

This is the very day God acted — let's celebrate and be festive! Salvation now, God. Salvation now! Oh yes, God — a free and full life! Blessed are you who enters in God's name, from God's house we bless you! God is God, he has bathed us in light. Adorn the shrine with garlands, hang colored banners above the altar!

You're my God, and I thank you. O my God, I lift high your praise. Thank God - he's so good. His love never quits!

When fear tried to set in, these words comforted me. Respectfully, I never want to take the word of God for granted. I don't know why, but I started to cry out to God for help. I felt in my spirit that this was bigger than what was being shared with society and the world. They had no answers, they were too proud to say "GOD, we need help," so many people perished, and they still continued to keep people in the dark. I didn't realize this until the Covid pandemic.

I started attending a church called Kingdom Builders in Brockton Massachusetts. This is where I first heard Apostle Naomi Burton, Bishop and Founder of Keys of the Kingdom tabernacle of prayer for all people INC Est, 1989 Brockton MA. The word of God that came out of her mouth was on point. She said, "you've got to be a HOLY GHOST RECEIVER." The Lord was dealing with me before I was going to Church. Now I go with expectancy. Most times, I would get ready to go to service. I would hear the LORD say a message, so I knew I had to be able to receive, letting me know there was going to be a word.

I could not move until the word was released. I couldn't move my feet, so I continued in worship where I sat, and then the word came forward. I told her the Lord spoke to me and said a word was coming forward and that was the reason why I was dragging my feet.

The very person that invited me to visit needed deliverance, and he answered her prayer. God began to deal with her, about some personal things. When the LORD gives you, an assignment, just do it, even if you don't understand. It's important to be spirit led at all times. It literally could mean life or death. I thank God for His word; it's always moving and abounding. I thank Him for not leaving me or forsaking me.

Galatians 6: 7-9 *Be not deceived; God is not mocked: for whatsoever a man soweth, that shall he also reap, for he that soweth to his flesh shall of the flesh reap corruption; but he that soweth to the Spirit shall of the Spirit reap life everlasting And let us not be weary in well doing, for in due season we shall reap, if we faint not.*

My sons Joseph and Raymond went up for prayer and Bishop Burton asked them who they were with, and they said they were with their mom. I went to the altar with them, and she began to minister to them both about some future turn of events, warnings, mostly for my younger son, and she asked me who I was. At that time, I really wasn't sure how to answer. I thought I was a prophet all this time, but that's not the office he called me to.

Bishop Harris told me that I needed to get a book, and that every time the Lord showed me or told me something, to write it down. He was going to begin to reveal things to me, but it was going to be for the body of Christ. God is going to tell me when to release it. I didn't know at that time if I was a prophet or not, then she asked, "who told you were a prophet?"" I said I just know," but I don't think I really understood what I was saying at the time. She told me I was released to be here. I said "okay." I didn't know how to answer her because I had no experience.

I enrolled in class in 2020 at New Destiny Prophetic Institute with Professor Dr. Prophet Felicia A Brown in Bear, Delaware, with much prayer and a lot of deliverance. Some things are clearer now. I feel God. I didn't realize how clouded my mind was until we had begun the lesson plan. It was so hard to receive. I couldn't process it as quickly as I would have liked to. I was having some issues with my memory due to stress from my marriage, my children, and my job. I was going through so much with my husband that the stress started to build up with no outlet, but it's over now we made it through the test and the storm. If we faint not, we shall reap!

Monica D Sylvester

TRUST THE PLAN

"For I know the plans I have for you, plans to prosper you and not to harm you, plans to give you hope and a future".

-Jeremiah 29:11

We normally associate plans with our typical arranging of dinner dates, school functions, doctors' appointments, vacations, and much more. As individuals, we are the ones deciding if these will work within the hustle of our daily life. We ask ourselves, "Do I have time? Will this interfere with another appointment? Do I feel like it? And is this within my budget?"; leaving the arranging and decision-making process all up to us. In doing this, we have full control (or at least we seem to think we do) over how we respond to the plans and outcomes we're setting. But how about this, do we ever seem to think about asking God what His plans are for our lives? Okay, we'll get to that in a moment. But before that, let me go back some to pre-COVID times.

In 2018, I was working for a company. I enjoyed my job but knew it would not be permanent. However, I was faithful, I always showed up and performed my required work duties, unsure of where this would lead me. As time passed, I begin to feel uneasy and unsettled, I started trying all that I could to get out of this job;

taking interviews for other jobs and completing applications that best fit my experience. This lasted for about two months. However, I had nowhere else to go and no other prospects. Unbeknownst to me, the supervisor position I applied for in 2018, just for kicks, which I did not get at the time, had just opened up as the young lady that did get the job was promoted. Well, I almost missed a God moment. I was so adamant on leaving because of the unsettling I was feeling; I thought it was God's way of telling me it was time to go. I initially turned down applying for the Supervisor position and kept searching. Well, I kept hearing God telling me to be patient as I was finding every way to take matters into my own hands. Not only did I hear God tell me to be patient, but I was also sensing great transition. Well, the deadline to apply for the Supervisor position was approaching, and I remember my manager coming to me saying, "Are you going to apply for the position, you will be a really great fit." At that point, I applied, but believed that I was going to be out of there soon anyway; mind you, I still had no prospects. I went along with the process of interviewing and was then offered the position. Needless to say, I accepted the offer and stayed with the company. What does this have to do with God's plans? Well, let me explain some more.

The year I accepted the offer as Supervisor was the same year, I ended up losing my job entirely. I was in this supervisory role for only about five months at this point, I was in the groove of things and just beginning to gain some level of comfort, well at least that's what I thought it was then. However, looking back, it was just the fact that I did my job because I knew how to do my job. I made sure I worked to the highest standards. At that time, I began mentally planning me and my family's life based on how far I could potentially grow within the company.

Interestingly enough, as much as I tried to "see" myself growing there, it still felt forced and unnatural. There was a part of me that was simply just not feeling it.

Well, one day, all the supervisors were called into a leadership meeting, where they advised us that the company had been bought out and we were losing our jobs within one month. I initially cried and was upset because I was thinking about how this could potentially affect my family, our bills, and my career. As the days and weeks went on, I began to attain peace about this transition, and left knowing my time with the company needed to come to an end. The situation in general put me in a place where I asked God, "When I felt transition in the first place and could not find another job, why did You let me go through a promotion to then have it all snatched up from under my feet?" Well, it didn't make sense then. However, I knew God was teaching me more and more about having faith, allowing my faith to increase, trusting the plans He has for me, while also understanding that I was to never gain comfort there in the first place.

Fast-forward some, since my faith was sincere, I just knew I was going to find a job within that first month of being unemployed. Well, umm, yea, no. That was not the case. In fact, I was unemployed for six months, only getting $600.00 a month in unemployment. Now, my husband was working, but my income was cut by almost three quarters of what I was making. Can somebody say FAVOR?! During this time, I not only believed God, but I put my faith in action. God began to build me up spiritually and mentally. I learned that just because I do not see what God promises when I think I ought to, it does not mean it will not manifest. God's timing is everything. I cannot stress that enough.

Now, because I was without work, I received a call from my mother-in-law when she told me the Hospital was hiring and provided me with an email address to send my resume. My mother-in-law did not even know who the person was whom I needed to send my resume to. She just happened to be on a casual call with someone and they inquired about me. They passed that email info to her to give to me. I am sure you are wondering what this has to do with anything, well just sit tight and keep reading. All I had was an email address, I did not know the person's name, what the position was, the salary, or the hours and benefits. If I could be honest, I was a bit hesitant about sending anything over, thinking it was about to be a waste of my time or that I was "probably not going to be a good fit." Just that quickly, I was about to miss out on opportunity and favor. Well, I felt an urgency in my spirit to submit my application immediately and not drag my feet on this one. I submitted it and went back to my daughter's class to continue volunteering. Not even ten minutes after I sent my resume, I received a phone call from the neurology department of the hospital offering me an interview that same week. How exciting was this?! I had tried for years to get into the hospital, and it never seemed to work for me, even though I had always been qualified for the positions. Because I wanted to remain in healthcare, I went to the interview, not knowing. I went in for one position but came out having been offered a position as a supervisor. Mind you, I had not yet completed an application, as this position was not even posted yet. Let's talk about FAVOR. I came into the position taking a major pay cut, but I knew I would be just fine. Especially since God had just come through when I was without work. God took great care of me and my family.

Fast-forward a couple of months, we were all hit with the pandemic, COVID-19. Oh, how all things changed during that time, work, school, church, and family. There were so many things we had to get adjusted to and acclimated with, which brought great frustration and change; some good and some not so good. Like the previous job I spoke of at the beginning, I began gaining traction with the company, and enjoyed what I was doing. I just knew I was going to move up the ladder, ultimately becoming a director within the company. Well, I can say I became quite comfortable, as my schedule and freedoms were just what I wanted, especially if I had to work for anyone. As time went on, I began to sense transition again, just as I did with my previous position. I began to deal with great opposition in my job, making what I was hired to do very hard. However, I stayed the course and began to trust that God was seeing me through. If I did not learn how to deal with different personalities before, I sure enough gained a crash course at that point. I felt so uneasy and unsettled that I found myself greatly disliking my place of employment. However, I refused to look for a new job, even when others suggested it. I hung in there and grasped even tighter to God. As I told myself, when my time is up here, He will make a way of escape for me. But what I ultimately felt was some sort of obligation to my position and to the supervisors. God had opened this door for me, so initially, I felt like I could not leave; at least not yet. That word 'patient' was all I kept hearing again, even though I knew transitioning was happening. All the while, I kept asking God, "Since this is where you have me positioned for now, what is my purpose for being here?" I was convinced there was a reason. As I think back, I could not figure out at the time as to why I was there. I am a firm believer that God does not have you positioned in places just for the fun of it, there is always a greater plan.

Here is to the greater plan that I could not see at the time. One day while at work, I happened to be walking into the break room where a board was positioned high up on the wall, there was some writing on it concerning shifts and some other things pertaining to time and staff schedules. Well, when I looked at the board, I saw "Making a Shift." Let me help you understand something, this board only had the word shift written on it, not the words "making a shift." At that point, I could not undo what I had just seen. I kept repeating it and asked God to help me understand what this was regarding. God caused a shift to take place in my life that very night, not even 5 hours later. A shift in my life concerning my eldest daughter. She had been dealing with depression, rejection, self-harm, rebellion, etc., and due to that, it was recommended she be sent to Rockford, which is a mental health facility. That evening, I had had enough, so I took out my blessed oil and laid my hands on her and began to pray. As I began to pray, my daughter began to have a demonic manifestation. Well, at that moment I felt as if I had failed her because fear gripped me — this was happening to my child! I did not feel well-equipped to handle what was happening before me. That is when the enemy wanted to make me feel that I was not a child of God, that I lacked authority and power in Him. Thank God for my spiritual mother and those around me who not only prayed and cared for my daughter, but also for me. I will expound on that testimony at a later date, as God is so amazing and so strategic. But what I did not know that day, something I know NOW, is God was preparing me, Johnita, for a shift to take place in my life that would get me to the place God needed me to be. When the shift happened, it felt like hell, but Hallelujah, Glory to God, He knew exactly what He was doing. I can honestly say that when I saw the words making a shift, I thought of something great and pleasing to the eyes, not knowing that God would take something that looked so ugly to my eyes and felt very unpleasant, so that He ultimately was the one who received the glory out of that situation. It took an uncomfortable and unfamiliar situation, one that caused me great uneasiness, to push me into purpose and to push me to be bold and confident in what He had called me to do. Never would I have imagined that God would set me up to be in position at this job to experience major shifting at the right time. Every day, minute, and second counted to get me to end up in that break room at my job to see those words on that very day. My God knows what He is doing every single time. Just as His time allows for us to know how strategically He moves. Where I am today has everything to do with how His plans are the best plans.

Remember in the beginning, I asked the question, "Do we ever seem to think about asking God what His plans are for our lives?" Not just for our future, but in our present which ultimately leads to our future. What an amazing question to ask, because even if we do find ourselves asking, how much of our lives are we trusting God with? Are we trying to manipulate the outcome or allowing God to be in control, even if it doesn't go the way we thought? He says "I know the plans I have for you. Well, even if we are allowing, God has an amazing way of setting up our paths, directing them towards the very plans He has for us. And while on the journey, He surely reminds us that His plans are certainly not to harm us, but to allow us to be prosperous, and to give us something to look forward to, expectation. He never said we would not feel some sort of discomfort, hurt, pain during the journey, but one thing He promises us for sure is that He will be our guide. When we allow God to lead, we will NEVER go wrong. He will always be there to rescue us from the discomfort, pain, hurt, and the unknown.

This is my walk with God and I will own it boldly! To Be Continued....

Johnita Calhoun

14-DAYS LIVING
WITH COVID-19

DAY 1

On Monday, November 30, 2020, I got off work and had my day planned as usual, I was feeling ok. The night before I had a little cough that went away. I thought it was from not blow-drying my hair when I had washed it the night before. So, I went to get my hair done, still feeling fine. When I finished, I worked all night, I never slept at all that day. So, I told my kids I was tired and not to bother me. I was going to take a nap. Monday is my normal day off. I was ready to go to sleep. I finally woke up and at 8pm went to the bathroom. I felt weird, but maybe I was still tired or something. So, I went back to sleep. Throughout the night I was getting hot and then very cold. I felt like my body was going through something. My body felt different. I tossed and turned uncomfortably. I could barely sleep. Woke up at 8:15 in the morning because I felt like I could not breathe. I tried to talk but felt like something was trying to stop me. I called my boss to let her know I was not feeling well. But as I was trying to talk to her, it felt like I was struggling to breathe and talk at the same time. I stood up and remember falling and hearing her ask if someone was at home with me. I could not even talk by this time. I was banging on my bedroom door. I knew my kids would come running to see what the noise was about. All I remember was seeing my children on their phone. Next thing, the EMTs were picking me up off the floor. I was on my way to Lourdes Hospital in Willingboro, New Jersey. As I entered the hospital, I saw all the nurses and doctors wearing their precautionary gear. They put me in a room with gray walls and lots of tape. It was an extra room they made for extra space to put people in. The nurse came in asking about what was going on and what I was experiencing. Do you have any symptoms? I told her what I was feeling and had been experiencing, like for example coughing, hot and cold chills, feeling weird all inside, I was having trouble breathing and had a headache. I was feeling like something was not right, I was struggling to breathe. She says, "it sounds like you have the symptoms of Covid-19, we will do a swab test through your nose, and it will take two to three days for the results." She then asked where I had been. I answered that I had only been at work and home. The nurse asked where I worked. I explained that I worked in an assisted living facility, and we had been getting tested every week. She then took my vitals. I had a fever of about 103 and my blood pressure was high, but that was to be expected. The doctor came in and said it looked like I may have Covid-19 symptoms, but they would let me know in a few days when my results came in. I would need to quarantine myself for 14 days.

"Is anyone in the home?"

"Yes," I told him, "My children."

"Is there a place where you can stay isolated?" he asked.

" Oh, yes." I started asking myself if this was really happening to me now. In my mind, I was so scared. I have seen so many people die from this sickness and saw what they had to go through, and now I had too also. The nurse gave me Tylenol and told me to get lots of rest. They sent me home to do the quarantine at home.

My aunt came to take me home after I called her, I was going to wait and let the ambulance take me, but the nurse said that the wait was 4 hours. I could not wait that long. The nurse helped me out and whipped me into the car. Of course, I sat in the back seat, not wanting to be close to my aunt, she was nervous and scared at the same time. She even rolled the windows down, cracking all four windows. I was laughing to keep from crying. The car ride was quiet besides her asking how I was feeling. I was feeling very weak. I told her I just wanted to lay down. She dropped me off and told me to go straight to my bedroom as if I were a little girl (laughing), but I sure did. I had to text my kids not to come by me nor bust in my room. I would be in my room quarantining with the door locked. It was late and I had no appetite nor was I able to drink. I just wanted to get in my bed. I managed to get in the shower. It felt like the longest shower ever because my breathing was short, and my body was weak. I took the Tylenol and put my PJs on, so I could get in the bed. After a while, I started to feel worse. I was going from hot to cold, and still had trouble breathing. Laying down to sitting up. "Oh my!" I thought" it is 9:30 at night and I am feeling warm air coming out of my mouth." I was going from cold to hot and hot to cold and sweating like crazy. I could not even sleep, tossing and turning all night. I was up all night. It felt like my clothes were getting soaking wet. I had to get up to change my clothes, feeling so weak, really feeling like life was being sucked out of me. I said to myself "how in the world am I going to make it through something like this?" How can anyone go through something this dangerous? Now I was scared to go to sleep, feeling like I would not wake up, something I or anyone close to me had never experienced before. I was the first one in many of my circles to have gotten this early on, all these things were going through my mind. The morning light was rising, I was awake, staring at the walls and looking out the window.

DAY 2

I had been up all night and my mind was racing. My fever had been high. My breathing was short, my body was aching, and I wasn't able to move as much or as fast as I would have liked at this point. My head was hurting. I really didn't care about trying to move around, feeling like crap at this point. All I could do was just lay there and look up at the ceiling and walls, praying that God would do a healing in this body quickly, because I needed it. Also, it was my birthday, it did not feel like it. I was stuck dealing with Covid-19. How crazy it was to be fighting this strange sickness that was turning the world upside down and hit me on my birthday. I was thinking how I was supposed to be in New York with a friend shopping, going out to dinner, having fun. But there I was in bed, sick as ever with tears running down my face. How could this be? How could it be that I was sick and stuck in this bed with Covid feeling at my lowest. But Then I said "God, I thank you because you gave me another year and another chance." I was reminded really quickly of God's grace and mercy. I was just having a moment. Sometimes, God will allow us to have a moment, but then he reminds us of all the times he was right there with us. I kept hearing my phone vibrate because of all the texting and calls. People were leaving messages to wish me a happy birthday. I was feeling so bad that I could not answer or respond because of how I was feeling and how weak I was.

DAY 3

I felt horrible, body aches and all. The only thing I barely had strength to do was to go to the bathroom which by now it wasn't very often, because I was not eating or drinking. I was still having shortness of breath. My chest was getting tight. I started crying because I felt so bad and helpless looking at those four walls with no sleep. It was 11 a.m. and something told me to look at my phone. I saw that Virtua Lourdes

Hospital had called. Today was the day my results were supposed to be in. So, I called the hospital. They give me the run-around. I explained to the operator that someone had called and told me to call back to the ER. Now, in my mind, I am like "I am sick and can barely breathe to talk, and now I have to do all this explaining?!" Finally, I was able to speak to a nurse who asked for all my personal information and then boom! She confirmed I had Covid-19. She then explained the quarantining rules and said she hoped I'd feel better. Was this the reality I was facing? How do people that are going through this sickness deal with it? These are the thoughts that were going through my mind. Feeling lonely and caring for yourself is hard, and I was trying to do it. All I could hear were the words of the doctor in my head. "You have Covid" and "just take Tylenol" as I was lying in bed. I still couldn't sleep. My kids were knocking on the door, checking on me, and I could barely talk, so I just tried to text them. But they would call my phone because I was texting too slowly for them. The tears started to roll down my face because this was feeling unfair. I was feeling helpless and could not do anything for myself. I was scared that death might have been knocking close to me. How could I have so much Faith while feeling like death was knocking so close at the door for me?

DAY 4

I felt like this was getting worse, the hot and cold chills, shaking, fever going up and down, my chest was so tight I could not breathe. I was struggling. I felt like I needed to go back to the hospital. So, I called 911 and the EMTs came. I told them I had a cold. It was hard for me to explain all the symptoms because I was trying to catch my breath. The EMTs took all my vitals. My blood pressure was high, my temperature was 102.8. The EMT said there was really nothing the hospital could do but they would still take me. In my head, I realized these are the same ones that came the first time. So, they put me in the chair and brought me down to the ambulance and when we got there the old man was explaining how there was not much that they could do. I just had to hang in there, these were the symptoms of Covid-19. I said I understood that, but something was wrong with my breathing and my chest. So, he went on and on till we got to the hospital. All I could do was pray that God would allow these nurses to help me figure out what was going on. They took me to a room, I figured it was the Quarantine section of the hospital. The nurse came in and took my vitals and as I was trying to explain what I was experiencing I could hardly talk; I just laid there waiting to see what was next. I was shaking so badly, trying to turn from one side to another, and it was uncomfortable, and breathing was difficult, all while happening at the same time. All I could think of in my mind was "God, please take all of this away and heal me." That is all I wanted him to do. The doctors came in and asked me how I was feeling. I was looking at him like, "dude, are you serious right now? You see me." So, they gave me Albuterol and did a chest x-ray which is a CT scan, the results came back that I had pneumonia as well. So now, with all these problems I was having, the doctor said they were discharging me, and I had to continue to quarantine, continue to take the Tylenol, and they added more medicine for me to take, which was the Albuterol. All I was concerned about was my breathing, I told the doctors, but he said the albuterol would open the airways to my lungs. So, I called for my kids' father to come pick me up. When he got there, I was waiting in the wheelchair. This gentleman nurse was so nice, he even helped me get into the truck and made sure that I was okay. As soon as I got in the car, the door was closed, and my children's father (BC) rolled the windows all the way down. Boy oh boy was he scared and nervous. This was the first time he had driven so fast. Never in my life had I ever seen him drive this fast. I was so scared for my life. But then in his mind he probably thought he had to get this girl out of this car (Lol). As we drove home, all I wanted to do was lay down. By now, I had been up for three and a half days. I felt so weak and tired. Going home, the drive was only 15 minutes. He did not even help me get out the car, but he made sure I got into that house and then told me to go straight to my room and then bed. I started to feel like I was a little kid as I was left there, I had a room to myself, but this was not right. I started to take all my medicine so I could stay on top, but I still felt the same.

DAY 5

I could not take feeling so helpless. I could not even help myself. My breathing was still bad. Doing everything the doctors told me to do, finally I was able to sleep for like 3 hours. I could not talk, I felt like my mind was going. All I could do was pray that God would heal me in that I was so scared for myself. I could barely move; I had aches and pains throughout my body. The light in my face was bothering me. It seemed like everything was hurting and bothering me all at the same time. All I could say in my mind was that something was not right. I know they say all this comes with Covid-19, I just felt there was more going on in my body. I still could not eat nor drink. By now my sense of smell and taste were going. My temperature was going up and down. I was still going through the hot and cold chills. Everyone was ringing my phone, but I just did not have the strength to do anything. I put my phone on silent since I could not do anything like talk or text. It felt like my health was spiraling out of control. It was mid-afternoon and I wanted to go back to the hospital because I felt like something was wrong. I was scared to go back because I might get the same EMTs again and I was tired of hearing the same thing. "There is nothing anybody can do, you have covid" that was getting on my nerves. Another thing was they may have sent me right back home. I said, "the heck with it," So, guess what? I called and got the same EMTs. They came into my bedroom while I was on the floor, got me up to help sit me in my rocking chair. They took my vitals and asked me what was going on today. I was trying to talk but had shortness of breath. Boom! They say again." You have Covid-19, these are the symptoms that come with this, there is no cure for Covid-19. There is nothing that the hospital can do." So, I got discouraged and just told them to leave, I was not going to go back to the hospital. He then said this was a process that I must go through. I was so upset because in my mind I knew that he was probably right, and I knew that if I went, they would just send me right back home. But then something came to my mind, and I said, "please just take me." I looked at their faces, and they looked angry, but all I could think of was "This Is My Health not yours," so they put me in the stretcher outside and got me to the hospital. While I was in the ambulance, the guy again told me I must let Covid take its course. I did not want to hear it. Then he said "I'm not trying to sound like I'm your father or drilling it into your head. I am just trying to explain to you and help you understand." We finally got to the hospital. They put me in the isolation room again. This time it seemed like the doctors and nurses were used to me, they saw I had been there quite a few times, so they took forever to come in. Finally, the nurse came in to measure my vitals and the doctor came in to check me and ask me what was wrong. I barely had a voice, so they said they would run some more tests. They did. An hour later they gave me medicine. The doctors came back and told me everything looked fine, I just had to stay in isolation. 'Just' I thought in disbelief. I was worried about my breathing. I told the doctors. All he said was that this is what Covid does, it attacks the airways into the lungs and that is what causes you to have shortness of breath. Back home for me again.

DAY 6

I was coming to realize that I was not going to get any help. I was trying to do everything and take all the medicine they said to take. But all I could do was lay there in my bed tossing and turning. My clothes were soaking wet, and my sheets were too. Trying to get out of the bed to change my clothes was a challenging thing to do. My sheets were wet also but all I could do was put a towel on top of the wet spot. That was how weak I was. I felt like it was a whole task because I felt so cold as I was trying to move. I was just like "oh no! I cannot do this." Each day seemed to get worse. But there was nothing I could do. Being isolated was getting to me, my mind was going everyday all day, a thousand miles per minute. I cried a lot because I was going through this by myself. Nobody knew that I was dealing with Covid. Only my kids and their father knew. But they were worried and scared as well for me and it seemed like it was starting to get to them as well, just by their voices on the phone. They were the only people I would answer my phone to because they knew I would just listen to them. My son would say "hold on mom, you are going to fight this Covid." Those words encouraged me. I was not drinking, nor even had a desire to eat or drink, but I did push myself to have a sip of water. If I needed something I would be on my own. Just looking around at my bedroom and the mess, I kept saying to myself "this room is going to need a deep cleaning." Clothes were piled up in baskets, with lots of clothes in bags from me changing my clothes constantly.

It was late, and I had to force myself to get up because my bed was completely wet, it was soaking through the towels as well. I started to cry because I was just too weak to do it, but I knew that it had to get done. I just did not have the strength, but I knew I could no longer lay in this bed like this. Thoughts playing in my mind about what everyone had been saying to me about this Covid illness, it made me just want to go back to the hospital, but I knew there was nothing they could do for me. Then trying to get back home as well was too much of a headache. It was a lot just praying to God to please help me because I knew this was a lot for me to go through.

DAY 7

It was Sunday. Normally I would be in prayer with my team if I were not sick with this Covid. But since I was sick, I had been praying a lot in my mind. I never thought feeling this lonely and helpless would affect me. All I kept saying to myself was that I am not alone, God is with me. Sometimes, in my spirit, I heard the worship songs playing in my head. I often found myself rocking to them and then the tears would fall down my face.

It seemed like every day was the same thing for me. It was so bright outside. It looked nice outside, but I knew it was getting cold because it was now the month of December. I felt like I was losing the dates and times, not knowing what day it was, trying to keep up, but unable. It seemed like the world was moving fast while I was stuck in this bed. The room seemed to be spinning in circles. One minute I was taking the covers off and the next I was putting them back on. My kids were texting me to check on me, but I felt like everything was annoying me at this point, feeling so stuck in this room. My stomach felt so empty I could feel it when I took sips of water, I could feel it go down into my stomach. Every breath I took became more difficult. This was the worst feeling someone could possibly go through — and do it alone with no one around to help you. During times like this, you have no choice but to encourage yourself and be strong for yourself. Suddenly, during the night, my coughing started to become a problem, I started to cough so hard. It felt like I was coughing up a lung and even my chest started to hurt to the point I was scared to cough. I was trying so hard not to cough. I would say to my thoughts now, "girl you know it's going to hurt " (Inside thought).

DAY 8

8 days on and I was still dealing with this virus, looking up at the ceiling. The light was coming in from the window, it was eight in the morning. I was still sick of trying to manage to get out this bed to try to take a shower. My voice was low as if I was losing my voice totally, but I was trying to breathe as I moved around to get my things together for my shower. As soon as I got in, I felt like I was going to pass out. My chest started to get tight, my nose felt like it was clogged up. So now in my mind I was like "hurry up and get out of the shower" because I started to not feel right. I leaned my head against the wall, and I tried to shower. I had never in my life taken a shower in 7 minutes, but I had to because I felt lightheaded and like I was going to pass out all at once. It took me forever, moving slowly because I was out of breath and coughing. As I sat in my recliner feeling bad, my phone started to ring. My prayer friends would call, and they would just pray with me as I listened in. I started to text my friends to tell them what I was dealing with and why I could not talk to them nor answer the calls. They were so worried, but I knew how they would get if they did not hear back from me. They already knew something was up when they had not heard from me, they had already started praying and interceding on my behalf. I talked to my friends every day. I only have a few I can count on my hand. To be honest, I was afraid and ashamed to be telling my friends that I was dealing with Covid because you hear all the stories of how people start to treat you differently when you have Covid. Yes, your friends may love you dearly, but that does not mean that they are not scared or worried about catching this virus. This virus has killed so many people. I have seen how

this virus has killed many people that I have known and patients that I took care of. You do not know all the details and facts about this Covid virus. Then people ask you all kinds of questions: how did you get it and where did you get it? The inside worries and then the looks. But my community of praying women and my spiritual mother did not treat me like that at all, they not only prayed, but helped to make sure if I needed anything they would provide it. And as I was laying down and my chest started to get tight. I really felt that this would be my last day. I was breathing harder and getting out of breath more quickly, I felt dizzy trying to catch my breath.

My phone rang, one of my prayer friends, Sammy, called me. I answered with a soft faint voice, but I was so out of breath I could not talk. Sammy told me I did not sound good at all, and she prayed with me. The tears rolled down my face because I knew it was good for me to hear another prayer. I was so scared to go back to the hospital. After praying, she started to cry. She said she was going to get me out of there and that I should not be scared, and this time would be different. Sammy called 911 and was put on hold; the dispatcher was on the other end. She started asking me questions. But when I tried to talk to the dispatcher, she knew something was wrong. Minutes later the EMT's were at my door. I sat there with a blank stare, praying, and hoping that it was not the same EMTs that came the last couple of times. My kids did not know how bad I was because they never saw me while I was sick. I did not want to scare them. But of course, when the paramedics came, they were wondering what was going on. Paramedics came in and took my vitals as they asked questions. Sammy was still on the phone the whole time the paramedics were there. The paramedics told Sammy that they were going to take me to a hospital and asked her what hospital she would like them to take me to. I told her Virtua Mount Holly. My vitals were super high, but it was because I was dealing with Covid. They even gave me oxygen, but my oxygen was low as well. "Do not worry! We have you and we are going to make sure you're well taken care of." That was a relief to hear. We arrived at the hospital, and I went into the ER Department. I was in and out of it, but I knew and saw a lot of people. They put me in an isolation room. It looked like a regular room to me. I was in so much pain. The nurse came in and asked me questions. They put the oxygen on me because they had to switch from the ambulance one. While the nurse was getting information into the computer, she started asking me questions, but then realized I could barely talk. The EMTs gave them the symptoms and what I was experiencing, and she noticed how bad my breathing was. She said she would wait a while until I could catch a breath and the oxygen had fully kicked in, she would come back to check on me. It was a while before they came back because I fell asleep and do not know how long I slept for. I had to sit up to get my blood work done and a lady was calling on my phone for me to get insurance information. I felt bombarded. Everything was happening so fast. About 15 minutes later, the nurse was back. "Hi, love how are you, how is your breathing? Are you breathing any better?" "So, my breathing is the same" I told her, "And I still have shortness of breath." I said, trying to catch my breath after every word. I felt the same. My vitals were still high. They began setting up to put in an IV for fluids. The doctor came in and I tried to explain to him what I had been going through. He even told me he was ordering some tests and getting an EKG and chest scan and all. By the evening, my blood work had come back but my blood level was extremely high. So, they had to draw more blood to see if there would be a change. About an hour later the doctor came in and told me he was glad I came in when I did, it did not look good. I could have died. I had blood clots on top of pneumonia and fluid around my lungs, so they admitted me. In my mind I was saying "I knew it all this time, something was wrong." Then he asked me if anyone from the hospital had told me about these issues when I had been seen on that previous Friday. I said "no, I told them about my breathing, that is what I have been concerned with all this time." As I sat waiting for a room, he started giving me all these medications through the IV.

DAY 9

A lady entered my room and told me she was there to get more blood work. I looked at the clock, it was 5:30 am. The nurse aides had been coming all night to do vitals and take my blood pressure. I had barely slept. The lady said they would be drawing blood as per the doctor's order every 3 hours. I was shocked, but hey what could I do? The nurse who cared for me was nice and sweet. She was there at 6 giving me a bunch of medicine and IV medicine too. After they gave me the medicine, I went right back to sleep. The doctors came to talk to me, but I was in and out, not knowing what they were saying to me. With all the medicines that I was getting through the IV and mouth, I did not even understand totally what they were saying to me. Eating was not a choice for me at this point, all I could do was sip on water. Finally, the nurse came in, all gowned up because I was in isolation, so nobody could come in the room without the proper PPE, which means Personal Protective Equipment. They looked like they were in space, but they had to take the proper precautions. I knew that because I worked in assisted living, and we had to wear it when someone was sick with Covid-19, so all this was not new to me. I told the nurses it was okay, no need to explain why they were wearing isolation gowns. They had to take my vitals, draw blood, check in, encourage me to eat and to ask how the pain was. Laying in the bed helpless, looking around at the walls, I had to start praying as I was thanking God, thanking him for allowing me to be here getting the help I need. I was so forever grateful. God spared my life yet another time. The tears started to fall because all I knew that it was nothing, but God's favor was on my life and his grace and mercy, that he loved me that much to save my life again. How awesome is our God? Despite how I was feeling, I was on God's mind.

DAY 10

Throughout the night, I was checked on by nurses and aides taking vital signs and doing blood work. I was in and out. I saw the sunlight rise and as grateful that God had spared my life. Being on oxygen and having IV's going through my arm, I could not believe this was my life right now. Having two arms with IV's running through with different medications in the bags was crazy. The doctors, nurses, and aides coming in were all dressed in gowns and masks, looking like outer space astronauts. I was taking so many oral pills as well without having any strength. The doctors came in to check on me, they only spent 45 seconds in the room, but I could understand their lives were at stake.

It was still hard for me to talk and breathe at the same time. Breakfast arrived, but I could only have liquid, I was on a special diet, but I could not drink the broth because my taste buds were so off. During the day, all I could do was sleep off and on. I was so worn out from all the other drugs I could not sleep. You would think because of all the medicines I was on I would be sleeping. Nope.

I was praying in my mind that this was my new life, this was my new life. The Lord was covering me though it all. I knew God's hand was all over me. I felt all the prayers that were going up on my behalf, because I was not afraid anymore, nor stressed or worried. I felt safe in his arms and knew that God's hand was on my life. I was even praying for the doctors and nurses and everyone that was helping me. God had my back, and he was making sure that the right people came into my room to care for me, the right people I needed.

DAY 11

As the nurse entered my room, she asked me how I was feeling and all I could say was I was ok and happy to be alive. She asked why I did not have the TV on. I told her I was in a place of comfort and peace and being in the presence of God. I would rather have my worship music on and be in prayer. I knew this was the time that God just wanted it to be me and him. So, I thought, this was the place and space he needed me to be in. It was just me and God. I was not going to sit here and feel sorry for myself and drown in this sickness. Staying in position was the hardest with the IV'S running through my arms, it was the hard trying to keep still. It was like God wanted me to stay still and stay in that position of prayer and worship. I would put prayer, worship music, the word, on at night. The lab tech came every three hours to draw blood. By the end of the night, my arms and hands were black, and blue with bruises. The Tech could not get a vein because as soon as the needle would go in, it would blow up like a balloon. They felt so bad to have to keep sticking me so many times. She was like, "I can't do this to you, this is too much for you." They waited a while to try again, but another lady came to do it, by then I felt like I was a poking doll. The nurse came in and laughed, "your veins are giving my Techs a problem "in her joking voice. "We are all trying to make the best out of this Covid situation, the number of people who have this virus is crazy" I told the nurse. Not being able to see family and friends and being alone was hard. But I had seen an aide sitting outside my room, I asked why she was sitting out there. She told me it was for my roommate; he was on suicide watch. My heart broke, and I started to feel some way. People are hurting and alone and do not have God. It's a lonely feeling and place. I immediately started to pray for my roommate. He would be yelling, screaming, cussing, and fussing. I started to pray even more for myself also.

DAY 12

I woke up to the Aide knocking at the door coming in. I looked at the clock, it was 5am. My aide had my medicine to give to me. I was getting used to the aides, nurses, and doctors coming into my room. I knew the times that they would come. I felt like I had their system and schedule down in my mind. There were many phone calls I needed to return, but I could not call everyone back. But by now I was able to text. I was staying up longer and trying to get into a routine. I felt the more I prayed and stayed in God's presence, the more I was regaining my strength. I was taking one day at a time, watching YouTube, video, and movies. That is all I could do. But my faith and trust in God was good and strong. After 1:30 on this day, the doctor came in again. He asked me how I felt. "You are looking much better." I said "OK" with a smile, happy on the inside because I knew what God was doing for me. I was fully awake and sitting up. That was good for me. He started to explain to me that my vitals were good, but my blood levels were high because of the Covid and all the other health issues I had. They were just going to continue to give the medicines but were going to increase some of them. All the people caring for me were so sweet and nice. I had the most helpful nurse aide. They were very understanding and sensitive. He then said, "you have not eaten; do you think you are ready, or can you try to?" I was hoping that I could taste the food, which was the problem I was having. I wanted to eat, and I was hungry. Every day was jello or broth, and tea. Ugh, I just do not like jello, the way it tastes and the texture. I had to figure out if I would be able to drink this broth and keep it down. So, my thought was trying to drink as much as I could. But I still could not taste the broth. It was crazy because my mind always tells me what is next to do, but it looked like I would be going back to sleep. It was either sleep, movies, worship, prayer or listening to the word. I knew the nurses and Aides would know every time they came into my room that I would have worship music on.

DAY 13

It seemed like each day I was there, that room was feeling more like my bedroom. Only, it did not have much, and my room was not decorated. Getting out of bed felt good, but only to go to the bathroom I was in a lot of pain while in transit. I had to take all the machines with me while going to the bathroom, hearing the alarms go off, and oh, every move I made something would go off. I felt like I had a little Independence, it felt good, especially because I was so used to doing everything for myself and moving to my own beat. I didn't like waiting on someone or asking for help to see if I could get up to move. While this was bothering me, the nurse came to ask if I was okay, one thing I can say is that the nurses who cared for me were the bomb. They were sweet and caring. But moving and getting up and down, boy oh boy, I would get so tired and out of breath quickly. I concentrated on doing one thing at a time, moving slowly like a turtle, no, more like a caterpillar I should say. That evening, the nurse told me they were going to put me on a regular diet to see if I could eat regular food. Oh, this time I felt as though I was ready, so I did soft food like tuna, crackers, and tea, things like that. For breakfast I would have oatmeal or cream of wheat, plain. Hospital food at Virtua was good. I did not care about the taste. I was hungry. I was not living in fear anymore when it came to trying the food, and that food was good. I no longer cared about the taste; I was hungry. I did not fear that the food had no taste, I just ate. You know, my thoughts were that this is my life right now, I must accept what it is.

DAY 14

Every day I would tell myself that people had gotten it worse than me. Covid has killed people, and it sucks. I thank God, he did not allow it to overtake me. But I was reminded that God had a purpose for my life, and I had to fight and push through it. I started to look at my life and people differently. I felt like God had given me another chance at life. So, the coughing, shortness of breath, blood clots water around my heart, and having pneumonia was not going to stop me. I knew that I had a long road to recovery, but I was okay. I know that I had a story to tell, people needed to know what I had experienced and how people were living with Covid-19 in silence. I had to tell it all. People are alone and lonely and do not want to talk about it or they are scared. But during these times, I was not lonely. God and His angels were camped all around me. I had my sisters in my powerhouse community, prayer warriors on my side with my spiritual mother who fasted and prayed with me on zoom for 21 days with my spiritual leaders. You must have people you can lean on and who have your back no matter what you are facing. I was able to use my voice and talk, and I thank God that I can talk a little longer. Now, I am an even better listener, because this was a time, I could not wait to tell it all in my story. I am okay because I lived with Covid-19, and I survived Covid-19. I am okay because God brought me through it. Now I can tell my story and someone else can share theirs without being in silence. I was living with Covid, and I am a Covid Survivor. Covid-19 did not beat me, I, and God, beat Covid-19.

Ronneisha Woodard

BIRTHING PAINS
IN TIME AND SPACE

The challenges of life often come by surprise, but in some cases, they are expected. Although many prophetic oracles of God foreshadowed the pandemic, the personal impact was underestimated and surprising. The pandemic thrust me into a phase that forced me to face avoided realities and uncover unhealed areas of my life.

Shortly before the pandemic occurred, I enrolled in a second master's program focusing on business administration. When I enrolled in the program, I initially believed the desire to obtain the degree derived from creating an additional income stream and, ultimately, changing professions. However, as the program neared its end, I discovered the journey was a misguided attempt to fill the unfulfilled feelings I was experiencing. The nagging unhappy feelings still existed when the program concluded. I spent a substantial amount of money, and time, to successfully complete the program to find out in the end, I still felt something was missing in my life. It was then I truly understood that I was unsuccessfully seeking fulfillment in various areas of my life.

Whilst enduring these emotions, and as the pandemic continued longer than anticipated, I was overwhelmingly consumed with the demands of remote teaching, the heavy workload of the graduate program, and existing in isolation from family and friends. I was forced to face who I was and discover more of who I had evolved into. At the start of the pandemic, the free time was significantly increased and tasks beyond the academic demands drastically lessened. Time was no longer consumed with the church, various appointments, and responsibilities. It appeared as if time had drastically slowed and the personal reflection in the mirror became more apparent. As I reflected and faced who I had evolved into, the previous years became a blur. It was as if time had stood still, and I could not truly identify who I was, my personal likes, and any progress that I had made in the unspoken goals that were the focus of my silent prayers.

The inescapable mirror of self-reflection and perception started to show me what time and space were hiding. I began to see myself as Jayna, the unfiltered version beyond the encouragement and accolades I was accustomed to receiving. I saw myself hiding behind my career, goals, and ministry. Over the years, I evolved into a people pleaser. I found myself doing things that I did not want to do to avoid disappointing others.

As the pandemic progressed and the end was nowhere in sight, the reflection in the mirror became more transparent. I could not fully identify who I indeed was outside of work, church, my inner circle of friends, and family. I discovered I had spent several years putting my internal desires aside to fulfill the image of what I believed was created by those who love me. I began to question if I had ever identified my own identity. I believe that in my young adulthood, I began to understand who I was created to be. As time passed, life did not evolve as I had expected, and my views of myself and God became distorted through disappointments. I lost sight of who I was and my purpose because with the passing of time, I began to believe my perception and life views were inaccurate. I started seeking answers and fulfillment in others. Living in isolation during the pandemic exposed my codependency on my family and inner circle. I no longer wanted to continue to live life dependent more on others than God.

I was in an internal tug-of war with myself to break from the codependency on others. I faced extreme challenges with putting myself first, mainly when I had to say no to people or be unavailable when they wanted my time and attention. I spent most of my days teaching 150 students remotely and simultaneously meeting the rigorous demands of the MBA program. I was overwhelmed. I simply did not have much more to give to others in time, space, and mental capacity. This presented a challenge to me as a people pleaser. It was incumbent upon me to learn to put myself first despite what others may feel I should do. I was determined to eliminate the codependency and do so silently. I did not believe I needed to announce to those around me about my codependent discovery and the daunting task of modifying the learned behavior. Although the feelings associated with the challenges I was facing were challenging, there was a feeling of the freedom of erecting boundaries. The boundaries erected an invisible fence around me that allowed space for God to truly step in. When the space was made, God stepped in, and the metamorphic experience commenced.

My analytic mind challenged the revelation of codependency. How could I be a firm believer in God, a faithful intercessor, and a prophetic scribe, and be codependent on others? How could I hear the voice of God clearly and not realize that I was leaning more on others than God? I discovered the truth in the scripture, Romans 11:29. God is not interested in revoking the gifts He has imparted into me. He is interested in my total deliverance so that those gifts can be effectively used. The pandemic facilitated my deliverance because God was finally able to have space to move the way He wanted to in my life.

The pandemic had created some level of silence and distance from others. I was home alone, facing the uncertainties of the pandemic and other areas. There were days when the uncertainties created fear as I faced everything in isolation. The once enjoyed silence in my home became uncomfortable and too loud. The silence that once signified a peaceful home began to represent loneliness and the magnified unfulfilled feelings. During this space and time, the reality and truth of my codependency on others was undeniably evident.

The pandemic not only brought loneliness and uncertainties, but also pain, fear, and grief. I had to watch family members physically fight COVID-19 powerlessly. As a family, we watched a beloved family member transition from cancer. A traditional funeral service was prohibited, and the mourning seemed to have been in isolation from each other. It all seemed unfair. I reverted to the thoughts and feelings of always being in mourning alone. In the past, I mourned my maternal grandmother, father, aunt, and uncle alone as I lived alone. I had family that mourned with me, but I always found myself alone, mourning as the grief continued.

Isolation was no longer desired or appreciated during the pandemic. I spent a considerable amount of time focusing on the pains of isolation until the Holy Spirit began to speak and remove the visual blinders and ear plugs. Once I opened myself up to the Holy Spirit and purposely ignored the distractions, there was an outpouring of love, wisdom, and direction. The sensitivity to the Holy Spirit was heightened. God began to speak about the time and season we were operating in. God divinely stepped in to get my attention to avoid misidentifying what was happening spiritually in the world and within myself. This was the time of breakthrough, healing, restoration, deliverance, elevation, and the time to manifest dreams and goals. The world was at a pause, but God allowed the remnant to continue moving and advancing.

Time and space allowed me to adopt a new self-perception that allowed me to see where I was mentally, spiritually, and emotionally. The mirror showed pieces of my life that seemed shattered, and I could not figure out a way to put the pieces back together. I needed God more than ever. I needed to hear and experience Him on a new level, desperately, because I began to question His love for me. Where was His power in the stubborn areas of my life that refused to change after constantly praying, fasting, and declaring His word? It was evident that my trust in God had drastically decreased because of time that appeared lost and wasted waiting for prayers to be answered. The unfulfilled feelings unlocked the truth of my suppressed feelings toward God. I covered up the evolving yet hidden place in my heart that I felt was broken by God. I worshiped and served God, all the while refusing to acknowledge what my heart was whispering. Then, one day, God asked me, "Why do you feel I have forsaken you?" That moment forced me to pause and face the avoided truth. The one-on-one, face-to-face encounter with God was imminent. The time had come to face another reality. I was discreetly angry with God.

Jayna Nowell

IN PURSUIT TO PUSH

I would have never thought I'd be carrying a child during a pandemic. Yes, I said it – pregnant…during a pandemic. I know you're sitting there thinking, well what was that like? Let me just say, I was 26 years old feeling like I was going through a midlife crisis. Let's take a trip down memory lane.

Every day it was just me, my developing baby, my thoughts, and my problems. This was just the beginning of the unknown. Not one of us knew what was to come next. At this time, I was at a point where I knew what I wanted in life, but I couldn't figure out for the life of me how to get there. All I knew is that I needed to get there before I gave birth to my daughter, but how could I get there while isolated? Yes COVID -19 caused the government to isolate us physically, but I was isolated mentally and spiritually as well. I felt alone. The thought of giving up came up time after time. I would constantly question if I really wanted to bring a child into the world at a time like this. I would sit at the side of my bed, frustrated with God, asking him for a sign or just a little guidance. I was also struggling financially; rent had backed up, utility bills were overdue, and accounts were over drafted. I was always toggling decisions. Do I pay my rent and leave and pay everything else next time? Do I pay the utility bill then rent? I couldn't figure it out. I had my own battle to fight, but instead I ran from it. I felt like every possible thing that could go wrong was going wrong. So many times, I thought of just leaving, and then I would remind myself you can't leave Kreah, we're in the middle of a pandemic; where are you going to go?

I had lost all motivation. I felt like I had no way out of this room of mine. Working from home didn't help at all. I'd roll out of my bed dreading to open up my laptop. Every day I would think to myself how making money wasn't helping my situation, it just felt like it wasn't enough. It got to the point we're I thought about quitting my job — while pregnant? "I'm just going to quit" "Why am I in this situation? This job isn't helping me." These thoughts lived freely in my head for months. Forgetting that this job was not only one of my biggest accomplishments, but a major blessing. I was a 26-year-old black girl working in a corporate leadership position and making a nice salary. I was in such a dark place that it didn't matter to me. I even began to distance myself from my friends. I didn't want anyone around me. I started to feel detached from everything and everyone. In my head, no one was doing anything to help me. I'd talk to them about their problems day in and day out. I'd help them give the best advice I could give while I was sitting there going through it myself. That right there caused me to remove myself from that equation. I asked myself why I was pouring into them when they're not pouring into me. Not realizing that they never knew I was going through anything. I kept my troubles to myself. Anyone that would ask how I was doing; I'd tell them I was doing well. But little did they know, behind that good was a bunch of hidden things: depression, anxiety, worry, anger. I even stopped my unborn child's father from coming around for a while. I was an emotional wreck. I isolated myself on all aspects of life. In my head I was living my life day in day out in an 11 by 15 sq ft room all alone.

There was one person that I could talk to and that was my favorite cousin. Oftentimes she and I would spend time thinking about what we wanted to do in the future. This one day she and I were on the phone just chatting and I happened to be venting to her moderately. I remember her saying "Friend, we gotta get it together, you're about to be a mom." That right there made me come to the realization that I was bottling all this stress and anger while carrying life. I thought to myself "my baby can feel everything that I'm feeling, I can't continue like this." I was literally miserable. I couldn't continue to sit in this funk. Each day she and I would spend more and more time discussing our lives and what we wanted to do. I began to jot goals down with her. I knew what I wanted to do. My only issue was that there were so many steps to take to get to my goals. One day my aunt, who you now known as Dr. Prophet Felicia Brown, asked me to help her get her PowerPoint slides together for her prophetic institute. I thought, she would be the perfect mentor for me. I have got to get it together, but I never asked her. I continued editing her PowerPoints whenever she needed. When she sent me something I'd get it done, proofread it and send it back. One day she asked me to add a slide for homework for her students. I read the homework:

> *"In the city where you live or where you're employed or attend church, can you identify what spirit is in operation? Is it a principality, power, rulers of the darkness, spiritual wickedness in high places? Can you discern?"*

I read it again and I thought to myself, "Oh this is deep." Whenever I'd edit anything for her, I would read over it to make sure everything looked okay, but this one topic caught my eye. For some reason I felt the urge to want to know more and hear this specific discussion. When I sent the PowerPoint back, I just had to ask her if I could jump in to hear this discussion; of course, she said yes. That night, she taught the class *How to identify specific spirits that may be assigned to families, regions, jobs, etc.* She advised the class that once they had identified these things, it would then tell them what to specifically pray for and against in their lives. She explained that she was there to teach them how to govern their territory and take back the atmosphere of homes, jobs, and churches. This right there taught me that I have authority over my atmosphere and that I no longer had to accept what was going on in my "region" (my home). This lesson brought light to my situation. From here I knew it was time to head down a different path. On this night, not only was there a light brought to my situation, but I was also introduced to the most anointed, gifted, God-fearing women whom I now call my sisters in Christ. I came off of this zoom with a different perspective.

Even after joining the zoom, I had not reached out to Prophet to be my mentor until one day she called me while I was working. Now, those of you who don't know, Felicia doesn't miss a beat! She called me on FaceTime staring at me with her big brown eyes and said, "Hey sweetie, how are you?" In my head I was like "Lord, what have you revealed to Aunty Dr. Prophet?!" The woman of God spoke these exact words "I had a dream, and in my dream, you were on a stage, and you were toggling decisions. There were a bunch of things on each stage exit, but it was as if you didn't know where to go" Yall! I hadn't spoken to her about anything, nor had my cousin (her daughter). I had only spoken to her about how she wanted those PowerPoint slides. My response to her was "can you be my mentor?" And she said to me, "You want me to be your spiritual mentor/coach or just a professional mentor; because you know, I'm not going to be "aunty", and this is going to stretch you." My stomach dropped because "aunty" is very delicate, and I knew that once she said I'm not going to be "aunty" I was getting Dr. Prophetic Felicia Brown in full form; but that's exactly who I needed. So, my response to her was "both."

"Both" was the start of a journey of newness. A fresh start, a new look at life. From this day forward I joined every prophetic institute zoom. Once that came to the end Prophet decided to take a small group of her mentees and form what we now call the Community. God had led Prophet to have us do a year of concentration and praying. We would meet on Zoom and pray and worship. I witnessed the spirit of God move through zoom every time we got together. For me, this was life changing. I had just separated myself from my friends and right before my eyes I had a new group of women in my life that would pray down fire. These ladies prayed me through my pregnancy. They took the "isolation" out of the pandemic for me. After every zoom I'd come off feeling so refreshed and ready to tackle anything. I was also learning how to pray myself. I began to get in the habit of praying every day and speaking life into my situation. Prophet was always big on declarations and declaring things over your life. "I declare and decree VICTORY over my life." "I declare and decree that this too shall pass." "I declare and decree that my current situation is not my final destination." "I decree and declare financial stability over my life." I had begun to speak these things over my life like prophet taught me. Each day I became more content with my situation because I knew God would see me through. Not only that, but I also knew that I had a community to spiritually back me up. This group of women were teaching me that prayer really does fix things. In the midst of all this, my landlord ended up reaching out to me to tell me that she did not need the full amount due and that she only wanted a small portion of it. I didn't just stop there, I continued to get on Zoom and meet with the community. I continued to fast and pray with them; because we were not only doing it for ourselves, but for our families and the things that were happening around us. We declared and decreed that the pandemic was not going to stop ANYTHING. Yes, the government ordered us to wear masks, but we declared that our mouths were not going to be muzzled. We were annihilating every plan, plot, and scheme of the enemy. And that was just the start of it.

You see, this pandemic spread more than just COVID-19. For me, it spread depression, anxiety, and a bunch of other things. I am proud to say that I beat every mental breakdown that was set out to destroy me while I carried life. I beat every attack that was set to make me give up. I can surely attest that what the devil meant for evil, God will turn for good. God will bring the right people into your life at the RIGHT time. To everyone out there, you are a breakthrough away from where God wants to take you. Position yourself and don't let the troubles of today break you.

Kreah Bailey

DEVELOPING
IN THE DARK

I chose "Developing in the dark" because most people alive, including me, most certainly have never been this way before. Never experienced anything remotely close to this type of disaster, the pandemic.

Some may not quite get the analogy of being developed in darkness unless you're a photographer or from a different era when photos had to go through a process of darkness to create the perfect picture. If you exposed the photo to light prematurely during the development stage/process, more than likely the photo would be ruined. Or if you kept it in the dark too long, the result would also be less than ideal.

The most remarkable thing about the developmental stage of **photographic processing or photographic development** is the chemical means by which photographic film or paper is treated after exposure to produce a negative or positive image. You could say the right chemical needs to be applied to get the desired results. Faith in reverse if you will. Because in the natural, we see the result we are aiming for, the intended goal. But you have to ensure the proper steps and the correct process is followed in order to get the desired results.

As a kingdom heir, we've been taught that each of us have already been "given" the wherewithal, the information and the authority to win. To do and be exactly who God predestined us to be. We have been preached to, and have studied it and read it to be more than conquerors, right? Yet 2020 shook us to the core. It took most out of their comfort level, their norm, removed their safety nets. We went from having the theory of the word, the formulas, being knowledgeable, to now having to walk out the word, experiencing what had been deposited in our spirit.

We had to question, was it a form of godliness and denying the power of God? Did we have a relationship with God beyond the four walls of the church? Kind of a spoiler alert, but any way, you end the story, we as kingdom heirs do win. We are in the world but not of the world. We have been given dual citizenship to have dominion in. But have the masses remembered what they've been taught?

If I was being brutally honest, this pandemic took me out of my spiritual/ Supernatural comfort parameters. I often rested in knowing God, knowing His will, His mind, His word, His movement. But when I looked up, I found myself in a place I'd NEVER been before. It kind of felt unsettling. For one, because I hadn't been given the heads-up, the foresight of the plight of the Pandemic better known as COVID-19. (I had to laugh at myself with the audacity of that statement and read myself like God did Job in 38:2. The Lord answered Job from the whirlwind: 2 "Who is this that questions my wisdom (the Omniscient All-Knowing God) by words without knowledge (comprehension)? 3 Brace yourself, because I have some questions for you, and you must answer them. 4 "Where were you when

I laid the foundations of the earth. Tell me if you know so much?")

Oh, I could try to ease my conscience by stating the obvious after the fact. But truthfully, I wasn't fully aware or prepared for the life altering pandemic *ugh. My life, our lives, would endure some things that were so horrific, depressing, debilitating, some literally gave up the ghost, and their fight for life.

As a leader, my experience was not just my personal experience but also for those in my charge. Pastoring, leading has a greater significance, a greater impact than anyone other than a leader could even imagine. And there was little to no time to develop into this "new normal." How do you speak "Peace" when people were panicking, losing it? Whole congregations infected with COVID; the numbers of deaths peaked each day. Someone you knew personally had it, survived it or died from it. We were in a place of perpetual mourning. The people expected a word from God. And they wanted it to be prophetic & precise. No one wanted hype without instruction and results. As a leader I had to be able to lead the people (Physically, Spiritually and Emotionally). I had to keep a watchful eye, listening ear, educating myself on health regimens, social awareness, mental health, resources, necessities, all while being spiritually in tune with the Spirit of the Living God, to navigate through these trying times.

Many things that were once our security system were no longer applicable. Disease, Deaths, Depression, Disloyalty, lack of commitment, lack of allegiance was all around. People were scrambling to keep their heads above the water. It was sheer {{PANIC}} in the onset of the pandemic. From the nation to the kingdom. It infiltrated into everyone's life.

At times, it was absolute hysteria. And the one place we've become accustomed to being, our safe haven, was no longer an option. In my lifetime, never would I have believed churches would be made/asked/coerced to close their doors. No, the government didn't have that much power, so I thought. I believe the rule of the shutdown became what we the Believers fell into, because we followed the narrative of the powers that be. And because of the power of media, the mega ministries (they demonstrated how we should move, and it spread like wildfire throughout the kingdom). You really had to be able to stand strong in your faith and what Father was speaking to "the Church." Most ministries closed their doors sometime in mid-March 2020 during the lockdown. Unfortunately, some have never re-opened.

Our lives and the way we knew them changed forever. One week we had "church" as usual, fellowshipping, greeting your neighbor, hugs, kisses, close communication, the next was a sterile, social distanced worship experience at best, if you returned to the building after the lockdown. The solution, virtual church. Who was really ready for virtual church? I personally was one who fought "VIRTUAL" Church tooth & nail. I was just socially awkward when it came to being in front of the camera. Now I had to voluntarily succumb to it.

The 20% of ministries that had budgets, media ministry, media business, cameras, equipment, staff, influencers, a payroll, etc., were able to adjust a little easier in that regard. But OMGoodness, God help the Mom & Pop ministries, and the other 80 %. How about those ministries that didn't have millennials or media savvy members who could navigate the internet or the likes of Zoom? It was "almost" humorous and woeful at the same time watching the baby boomers do live services on social media, zoom, stream yard, etc. Some didn't have cameras, just mobile devices, tablets, or iPads. And it felt like the internet was not willing to cooperate. From slow, to no connection, getting a good service became difficult some weeks.

Many made their best attempt of live services, teaching/preaching while seated on their living room sofa, in 3-piece suits, wearing their "church" hats, and believe it or not, preaching in robes. After a while, that type of dress code stopped. And people became more relaxed in their dress. There were misplaced phone angles, we looked up so many noses and saw too many double chins. (Lord help your people). After a while, some got it together and others didn't care, or just gave up virtual services, and resorted to "phone church," prayer lines, and even conferences via the phone.

Talk about scrambling to keep the ministry members together. Honestly trying to keep the people connected, engaged, encouraged, edified, and hopeful. Many found their strength in our weekly gatherings, be it prayer, Bible Study, Fellowships, or Sunday Services.

I look back and ask; HOW did we build media ministry so expeditiously? Because my concern at the onset was, how do you build and maintain a media ministry that is advantageous to the covenant members? Because I was determined to give the members the type of services, they were accustomed to. I didn't want to cut them short. Then the logistics hit me. Nothing is free. How are the financial needs going to be met? We're not coming in the building, we only have online services, how do you do online giving? So, then the dilemma, unfortunately was "finances." Even with the doors closed, the mortgage, and every other expense still needed to be met.

Watch this, through this pandemic, I found out, out of sight, out of mind. Someone with good intentions said to me, "church just ain't that important to most people anymore." Wow, I pondered those words, could that be true? Or was the local ministry not that important anymore. But to be fair, and looking at things logically, perhaps some wanted out but didn't know how to get out. Was this pandemic a way of escape they'd been looking for?

I understood the statement, but my hope as a leader was that people were keeping their connection with God. That they were maintaining their foundational truths, practices, and principles. The very things, ways and acts that kept us (prayer, fasting, confessions, reading, reciting, recalling the word, psalms/singing, praise, worship, fellowship). Because it is what I pulled from, what I taught. It's what I knew worked. Tried and true. I Individually, and then corporately, put us on fasts. We had purposeful prayer groups, prayer schedules, prayer services, and more fasting with prayer. I understood if we're not to faint, we must pray.

Thankfully, Father graced the ministry with great sons and daughters that pulled up their sleeves to work in ministry. When you don't have a large ministry to start with, and then add the pandemic, we suffer from attrition in numbers. Talking about developing in the dark. Some who stepped up weren't really visible prepandemic. And some simply stepped up in their skill set, gifts, stability, accountability, responsibility, devotion, etc. We needed help in the sanctuary and Father was supplying the need. He was downloading with intel from heaven. We began to operate in new grids of graces. His Spirit was literally teaching us to operate in His capacity. For things we weren't sure about, we found help or help found us. Within one week, we developed a media ministry, so that our covenant family could continue to fellowship together. Was it perfect? Absolutely not. When I tell you the growing pains, in just the lighting, it's not as easy as some believe. (With my color and the rest of the people on the platform good and brown. God Bless Production!)

Can I be the first to say? Online ministry/service is different. People have opinions, and they voice them right online, during the service. Oh, and don't forget the scammers who come on soliciting money from the viewers.

Ministry isn't for the weak, or faint at heart. People critique and criticize you and the ministry. Things you wouldn't even pay attention to. It was strange to me. People have opinions about what you preach, how you preach, what you wear, how you look, how you stand, shout, dance, y'all praise too much, y'all worship too long, if you receive tithe, offerings, or seed for the ministry, there's a complaint, the music's too loud, the praise team isn't color coordinated, the graphics, the lighting, everything! And I mean EVERYTHING!

Honestly speaking, virtual and media ministry has stretched me as a person, but most importantly spiritually. There is a greater compassion and sensitivity for people. One thing among many things I noted and enjoyed about media ministry was the capacity to reach people. I know I would have never had the opportunity to minister to so many different types of people, from all walks of life, denominations to no denomination, from the saved to the unsaved. I understood my reach, my assignment, and the severity of the times we were living in. Most of us went to international ministries overnight. It was mind-blowing. And to really get feedback and testimonies from various parts of the world was fascinating.

My spiritual senses were elevated, if I can say it like that. Talk about bout the Supernatural experiences, I was amazed how the gifts in the Spirit were heightened when I was ministering. As soon as I begin to look into the camera, it was as if I was transported into other dimensions. I had never experienced anything remotely close to those experiences. It was such a surety in the Spirit. It was the most amazing thing while we were on lockdown, we pre-recorded the services 2 at a time, whew. Father gave this "Ole Doll" the strength in the body what the spirit was willing. That was the Lord's Grace upon me, each Thursday, "essential personnel," and I scurried in the Temple and had full on "church" as if the place was packed with praising, worshipping, fellowshipping, and expectant congregants. God was in the place for sure, and when the services aired, the Spirit of the Lord was palpable. I loved getting the testimonies of how the sermon and/or service was timely and met the viewers' needs and expectations.

his has been a faith walk! We had to be able to work within capacity and zero extra budget. God blessed our Covenant sons and daughters to be a blessing and ministry pulled from somewhere to get the necessities to operate. I learned how to navigate Zoom & Facebook live to do weekly Bible Study, counseling sessions, pre-marital counseling, ministry meetings of every type, even 2 Ministerial School and Training Classes (Graduating a Class in November 2021). Having to be creative for fellowships and anything we would normally do in person, we would now utilize Zoom, whew!

Our HOPE Ministry expanded by 100%. The doors NEVER closed. We opened every week. We learned how to do everything safely, social distancing, putting the food in to go cartons, picking up outside. Our HOPE Ministry made connections and donations were at a surplus. We kept decreeing and declaring the Joseph Anointing/The Joseph Effect, Blessed to be a Blessing. Literally, we had so much, we furnished food to three other ministries, including dropping off food in another county.

We learned to Believe God for everything, in everything. His Peace, Protection, Provision/Prosperity. We Believed for divine health, healing, hope, and help. I had to believe & receive from God for the intel/answers for not only me and my family, but also for those in my charge. For the Spiritual, Emotional, Psychological, and Physical. And at times Living out "Moses where is your God"? We need answers! We need help! And even though it may have gotten dark, and some steps took more faith than others, God processed, developed and delivered His promises.

Jeremiah 29:11 *For I know the plans I have for you, declares the Lord, plans to prosper you and not to harm you, plans to give you hope and a future.*

Apostle Sharon R. Robinson

SUMMARY

Coronavirus has brought much of what used to constitute daily life to a screeching halt. Wherever you find yourself, there is a miracle in Perseverance. If you're toggling between decisions, don't stay in the valley deciding too long and become stagnant, don't worry whether it'll be right or wrong, just make a move. Trust the Lord will nudge you if it's the wrong decision. Trust God's plan for your life knowing he promised an expected end. When you're feeling those birthing pain, push, and you will see a divine restart and will sense something magnificent is about to happen, what literally took years will only take weeks, days, or seconds. Being developed in the dark will have you stepping out of your comfort zone. It will be the best thing that has ever happened. Yes, you can and will prosper during this pandemic.

Ask me how I know!

CHRONICLES BIO

Kreah K. Bailey resides in Boston, MA. She is the manager of a Call Center in the healthcare industry. She is an aspiring leader who recognizes and values upward mobility.

* * *

Johnita Calhoun is a proud wife and mother. She holds a bachelor's degree of Liberal Arts and has ten years' experience in healthcare. Her true passion is to help those in need. Johnita is the Founder and CEO of All Things P'Youre; a brand that ensures cleanliness and pureness of products for one's skin.

* * *

Ronneisha Woodard is a Home Health Aide/Med-Tech technician. She is also the CEO of Gifted Caring Hands Private Agency. She currently resides in Riverside, NJ. Her goal is to expand her business to many locations around the states, helping the elderly live a comfortable life in the comfort of their homes. She wants to let young women like herself know about the struggles she endured, and that God is faithful, and he will bring us out of every trial. Life will throw things at you, but it's how you handle it that's important. Life struggles will make you stronger. Trust God and all his promises will come to pass.

* * *

Marsha Jacintha Joseph was born and raised in Boston, MA. She is a first generation American, her family hailing from Antigua and Dominica, small islands in The West Indies. Marsha is a graduate of Northeastern University and is continuing her education at Southern New Hampshire University. She is a poet, spoken word artist, a recording artist, an author and a prophet. Marsha has traveled all around the United States performing and ministering to youth groups, women's conventions, and churches. Marsha is also an entrepreneur and the owner of Marsha Jacintha's Creations, where she uses her gifts to empower and inspire.

* * *

Jayna Nowell is a licensed minister, educator, and Prophetic Scribe. She serves as the Prophetic Scribe for FAB Impact Ministry Company of Prophets. Jayna resides in Wilmington, DE. She holds a BS in Elementary Education, MS in Educational Leadership, and Master of Business Administration.

* * *

Tyeast Amankwah is an ordained minister of the Gospel of Jesus Christ. She holds a Bachelor of Arts in Christian Ministry and Associates in Theology. Tyeast is currently a professional in the field of Parks and Recreation where she works as a Park Superintendent managing local and state parks. She is also a Certified Event Associate in Events Management. She resides in Wilmington, Delaware.

* * *

Joi' Jno-Baptiste is an American Author who resides in New Jersey. She is a wife and mother. She earned her bachelor's degree in psychology, and she has 16 years' experience in the Human Services field. Joi' has a passion for helping others.

* * *

Monica Devon Sylvester was born February 28, 1969, in Baltimore, Maryland and raised in Kinston, North Carolina until her family moved to Boston, Massachusetts around the age of five. She has been a wife for twenty-seven years and a mom for over thirty-six years. Monica knows that she gave birth to seven wonderful children, but GOD gave them life. She has four beautiful grandchildren whom she loves dearly.

I was young and now I am old, yet I have never seen the righteous forsaken nor his seed begging bread Psalm 37:25kjv.

God is not a man, that he should lie; neither the son of man, that he should repent: hath he said, and shall he not do it? Or hath he spoken, and shall he not make it good? Numbers 23:19

"I Still have HOPE and FAITH in EVERY word GOD says. AMEN"

* * *

Cheryl McLeod is an American educator and *new* inventor. She holds a BA in English, and an MS in Management and Leadership. Cheryl is the proud owner of CATASH Collections, LLC, a company that offers unique Tailored Greeting products (New Jersey). She is also the founder of the Shakespeare Leadership Academy, a NJ nonprofit private co-educational Christian preparatory school that operates for the advancement of the culture of the Kingdom of GOD!

* * *

Theresa John-Menefee is a Minister, Evangelist, Prophetic Intercessor. Born and raised in Boston, Massachusetts, she currently resides in Newark, DE. Theresa has over 32 years of Administrative and Human Resource experience and 8 years of Property Management and Real

Estate experience. She is also a Culinary Artist, Private/Personal Chef and Caterer, and currently serves as Executive overseer of Administrators, Liaison, and adjutants for F.A.B. Impact Ministries. She is grateful for having done all these things thanks to the Glory of God.

* * *

Apostle Sharon R. Robinson is a mother, Kingdom heir, and works in the Five-fold ministry in the Lord's Church. She is the Senior Lead Servant & Founder of **New Jerusalem Temple of the Living God, West Collingswood, New Jersey**.